Win Your First Y
Teaching Middle School

MW00560330

Feel empowered during your first year of teaching middle school by applying the concise tips and tools in this book.

Author Stephen Katzel shows you how to create an effective system to structure your classroom, implement daily routines, plan for the short and long term, utilize technology, communicate well with parents, handle formal and informal observations, and move up the salary scale. He also shares advice on relating to the unique needs of middle schoolers, handling difficult supervisors or coworkers, and adapting to change.

Perfect for beginning middle school or junior high teachers, the book offers strategies and templates you can use immediately to kick start a successful teaching career.

Stephen Katzel currently lives in Rockville, Maryland. He is a team leader and a middle school social studies teacher. Along with writing, he enjoys hiking, playing baseball, running, and traveling the country.

Also Available from Routledge
Eye On Education
(www.routledge.com/k-12)

Our Diverse Middle School Students:
A Guide to Equitable and Responsive Teaching
Elizabeth D. Dore and Deborah H. McMurtrie

Everyday SEL in Middle School:
Integrating Social-Emotional Learning and Mindfulness
Into Your Classroom
Carla Tantillo Philibert

Working Hard, Working Happy:
Cultivating a Culture of Effort and Joy
in the Classroom
Rita Platt

Two Teachers in the Room:
Strategies for Co-Teaching Success
Elizabeth Stein

Authentic Assessment in Social Studies:
A Guide to Keeping It Real
David Sherrin

The Elements of Education for Teachers:
50 Research-Based Principles Every Educator Should Know
Austin Volz, Julia Higdon, William Lidwell

Classroom Management from the Ground Up
Todd Whitaker, Katherine Whitaker, Madeline Whitaker Good

10 Keys to Student Empowerment:
Unlocking the Hero in Each Child
Cathleen Beachboard and Marynn Dause

Win Your First Year of Teaching Middle School

Strategies and Tools for Success

Stephen Katzel

Routledge
Taylor & Francis Group

NEW YORK AND LONDON

First published 2021
by Routledge
52 Vanderbilt Avenue, New York, NY 10017

and by Routledge
2 Park Square, Milton Park, Abingdon, Oxon, OX14 4RN

Routledge is an imprint of the Taylor & Francis Group, an informa business

© 2021 Stephen Katzel

The right of Stephen Katzel to be identified as author of this work has been asserted by him in accordance with sections 77 and 78 of the Copyright, Designs and Patents Act 1988.

All rights reserved. No part of this book may be reprinted or reproduced or utilised in any form or by any electronic, mechanical, or other means, now known or hereafter invented, including photocopying and recording, or in any information storage or retrieval system, without permission in writing from the publishers.

Trademark notice: Product or corporate names may be trademarks or registered trademarks, and are used only for identification and explanation without intent to infringe.

Library of Congress Cataloging-in-Publication Data
A catalog record for this title has been requested

ISBN: 978-0-367-74295-9 (hbk)
ISBN: 978-0-367-74148-8 (pbk)
ISBN: 978-1-003-15698-7 (ebk)

Typeset in Palatino
by SPi Global, India

This book is humbly dedicated to first-year teachers.

Contents

About the Author

Stephen Katzel currently lives in Rockville, Maryland. He is a team leader and a middle school social studies teacher. Along with writing, he enjoys hiking, playing baseball, running, and traveling the country.

Acknowledgements

I am eternally grateful to my parents, who have supported me in any endeavor I have pursued. I would also like to thank Angela, who has supported me throughout the process of writing this book.

Introduction

The purpose of this book is to provide practical advice and tips to first-year teachers in the new digital age. The educational topics and content that you learned in college serve as a foundation for you to start teaching. Staying current with pedagogy and the newest "educational jargon" is important while learning in college and while completing your student teaching experience. However, discussing the most up-to-date pedagogy and jargon with peers and professors differs from implementing them into your classroom. While conversations with peers and professors are important, new teachers learn best when they implement actionable ideas from their own winning system. Transitioning form learning about teaching to having a class of your own is one of the most exciting moments in your career. The purpose of this book is to give you, and all other first-year teachers, applicable strategies and advice that you can use in your classroom from your first day as a teacher, and beyond. My goal is to empower each first-year teacher with the tools and methods to "win" their first year of teaching. The system that I developed was a direct result of the trials and tribulations I faced as a first-year teacher. I started as a first-year teacher in a suburb of Phoenix, Arizona. My teaching career then brought me back to my home state of Maryland, right outside of Washington, DC.

Currently, I teach in a school that is very high achieving and has only a small population of low-income students. However, in the first four years of my teaching experience I taught in predominantly low-income schools, which gives me a unique perspective on how low-income and high-income schools differ. I have a general education and special education background, which furthers my credibility in understanding the struggles of a first-year teacher in either realm. I am currently a team leader and teach social studies. Part of my role as a supervisor is working with teachers across all subjects. I have a strong belief that developing a winning system allows first-year teachers to be successful in any subject that they teach. This book encompasses all of the advice I want to give first-year teachers to help them in their transition to teaching. The emphasis of this book is on applicable actions and methods that you can use to make your life easier during your first year. Throughout my career, I have constantly taken professional development courses and have over seventy-five post-baccalaureate credits in addition to my graduate degree. While taking classes to learn new teaching strategies is extremely important, applying those newly learned skills with ease in front of a class of thirty students requires having a winning system in place. Developing such a system requires first-year teachers to reflect on their experiences and strengths.

I believe that my perspective provides a fresh and unique outlook on education and how first-year teachers can adapt their own styles to my winning system. There were several factors that led to me writing this book. In my first year of teaching, I felt lost and overwhelmed, for a variety of reasons. I had little support in my transition from a student-teacher to a first-year teacher, and wish I'd had more direction or a "playbook." I view my book as a "playbook" for first-year teachers to use in their classroom in a variety of areas concerning education. Too many educational resources are hundreds of pages long and give an overwhelming amount of information. During my first year of teaching, I did not have the time or energy to read textbooks that were long and formulaic. Keeping these factors in mind, I was intentional about what topics are discussed in this book, and the length as well. Your time is valuable, and I intend for you to get something out of each page of this book. As a new teacher, you will learn a new curriculum, meet new coworkers, run a classroom, grade papers, answer emails, and so much more. Making time to read a textbook of more than five hundred pages would be difficult to pull off during the first month of school, or even during the summer for that matter. The advice I give is relevant, practical, centered around common sense, and focuses on using technology efficiently.

Success as a first year teacher is an arbitrary metric to measure for a multitude of reasons. Since "success" can be measured differently depending on the individual, I challenge you to come up with your own definition of what "success" looks like for you. In my opinion, knowing strategies for classroom management, planning, and utilizing technology are all signs of a successful first year. I delve further into these topics later on in the book. This involves developing your own "winning system," which will help guide you to a successful first year. The value of this book is that you will have a playbook to refer to throughout your first year. I am a firm believer that you learn things best once you do them yourself. I give you concrete examples and methods to structure your classroom. Ultimately, this book will be the spark to jumpstart your first year of teaching.

The journey of a first-year teacher is always exiting and full of surprises. I feel that this line is very clichéd, but it is true! In my first year of teaching, I received a lot of criticisms, but not many action steps to remedy my shortcomings. One of my supervisors was ineffective and constantly gave harsh criticisms without any substantial feedback. I was told "that does not work" and I started to dread observations and feedback. They were harsh and could have easily made me feel disillusioned with teaching altogether. I hope that you do not have a horrible supervisor, but this is an unfortunate possibility in any job or profession. I decided that no matter how harsh their critiques of my lessons, I would improve. Some of the feedback was downright ridiculous, such as criticizing how I said "Good Morning" to students. Yet some of their feedback was valid and helped me grow as an educator. The significant growth I experienced as an educator began when I started developing my own winning system. No matter what your circumstances are in your first year, persevere, adapt, and overcome. I wish I had a set of tools or a playbook to refer to during my first year of teaching to help guide me, as it would have made this year of teaching more enjoyable. And, ultimately, it would have made my first year more conducive for student learning. On top of an ineffective supervisor, there was a 1,000-page copy limit per month! That severely hampered my lessons and my ideas for teaching, but I made it work. I had to get creative and take risks with the planning and delivery of content. Some of the risks did not pay off and ended poorly, while others paid dividends. Again, what I am getting at is that, no matter what your circumstances in your first year, you must adapt and overcome. Use this book to guide your decision making to alleviate the pressure of being a first-year teacher. You are going to do an amazing job, and this will be one of the most exciting experiences in your career. Seize the year, seize the day, and seize every moment. You are going to "win" your first year of teaching!

1

Set Up a Winning System

Any classroom experience you've had before your first year of "official" teaching is only a small piece of the puzzle. Student teaching and volunteering in a classroom is useful experience since you get to watch an experienced educator in action. Ideally, you observed what systems the teacher had in place and the pros/cons of their system. Whether your mentor teacher knew it or not, they had their own system wherein they (hopefully) had a structure for management and student achievement. Hopefully, each first-year teacher has witnessed a "winning" system in action. Classroom rules for instruction and behavior (behavior management), expectations (behavioral solutions), and routines (structure) are the three pillars to a "winning system." My definition of a "winning system" doesn't come from a textbook or course. It comes from real-life experiences in the classroom and countless hours observing other teachers perform lessons. A winning system in one classroom can look entirely different than a winning system in another classroom. There is no "one size fits all" system. However, winning systems all have variations of the three pillars in common. Without behavior management, there is no mutual respect among students and teachers. Without expectations, students will not know how to behave in the classroom. Without routines, students will feel that their class is unpredictable day to day. Regardless of how a winning system is structured, the ultimate goal for each teacher is student achievement and learning. It does not matter what type of classroom I walk into; I know what good teaching looks like and what student learning looks like. I can walk into a French classroom and see within 5 minutes if a teacher has a winning system. I do not speak French, but I can observe student and teacher behaviors.

A closer look at the three pillars:

- **Behavior management** is how a teacher responds to the student's behavior and misbehavior. If a student calls out or misbehaves, does the teacher yell? Do they pull the student aside to talk? Do they ignore the behavior completely? If a student does something positive, does the teacher praise them? Does the teacher recognize when a student does something positive? Behavior management is essentially how an educator responds to the actions of their students.
- **Expectations** are whether the teacher believes that their students can grow. Does the teacher set clear expectations for their class? Do students raise their hand or call out?
- **Routines (structure)** are extremely important to consider as well. Do students know what to do when they walk in, walk out, work independently, or work with others? These are important questions that must be clearly answered and established in a teacher's first year.

A "winning system" is a classroom where students have high expectations of themselves, know what to expect each day, clearly know the rules of the classroom, respect their teacher, respect their peers, succeed academically, and are not scared to take risks. None of the previously mentioned things are possible without having a plan to get there! However, first-year teachers must set up their own "winning system" that is molded to their personality and teaching style. A new teacher's style will be molded through the three pillars of the system. How a first-year teacher approaches behavior management, expectations, and routines is critical in the development of a winning system. The system focuses on the core beliefs, values, and goals that a teacher establishes for their students and for themselves. To circle back to my first point, typically your classroom experiences prior to your own class/classes are as a guest in the classroom. For better or for worse, the mentor teacher you are shadowing has already set the tone in their classroom, which will shape how the students in the room view the teacher and themselves as learners.

Whether the system is a "winning" one depends on the teacher. It is imperative for first-year teachers to reflect on the systems that they have seen in classrooms they have been a part of. First-year teachers should reflect on their experiences to see what parts of any system they want to use, and what they do not want to use, in their own classroom. Typically, a first-year teacher has had a student teaching experience with a "mentor teacher" who helped

Mentor Teacher Checklist (Example)

Question	Evidence (Lessons, Management Strategies, ext.)
What did my mentor teacher do well?	1. Many lessons were content, and teacher based 2. Had routine for start, middle, and end of class 3. Classroom management was consistent and clear
What could my mentor teacher improve in their classroom?	1. Create more lessons that are student-centered and promote student discourse 2. Have a clear I do, we do, you do when going over assignments 3. Make directions clearer when going over class assignments
What strategies and parts of the teachers' system could improve?	1. Have clearer expectations on what to do when a student is absent 2. Post whether or not there is homework on the board
Does my mentor teacher even have a system in place? If the teacher has a system in place, is it a winning system?	1. My mentor teacher did have a system in place. It was a winning system due to the procedures, expectations, routines, and rules that were clearly established well before my time in their classroom. It was easy for me to jump in as a guest teacher and teach the students.

Figure 1.1 Example of a mentor-teacher checklist. (A checklist that allows for first-year teachers to write down if the teacher they were paired with during student teaching had a winning system and what strengths/weaknesses their mentor teacher had.)

them learn how to teach. This experience can range from a period as short as eight weeks to as long as an entire school year. (Figure 1.1).

A winning system is a collection of actions that a teacher makes on a daily basis that must be maintained throughout the entire school year. Ideally, the teacher sets the foundation of the winning system on the first day of school and reinforces the system throughout the first week of school. This kind of system does not happen overnight and requires a well-thought-out plan that includes classroom rules for instruction, behavior (behavior management), expectations (behavioral solutions), and routines (structure). Having a well-thought-out plan encompassing those three ideas will ultimately lead to high student engagement, high student achievement, clear classroom rules, and well-established routines.

Creating Structure and Routines

Having a structured classroom is arguably the most important step in establishing a winning system. Regardless of whether a student is in first grade or twelfth grade, they crave structure and consistency in any classroom they are in. The following observations do not come from a particular study, college course, or textbook. My opinions on classroom structure are drawn solely from my experiences teaching middle school students. Students do not like to walk into a room and have different procedures and rules each and every day. They will not know what is expected in terms of their behavior. A first-year teacher should have a set of routines that are established the first week of school and, more importantly, maintained throughout the **entire school year.** Students should know the routine for when they enter the classroom, which requires multiple steps. The first step is that a teacher should have the date, objective, "do now" (for example, a set of directions on what papers to pick up, what papers to take out, or to grab a laptop from the cart), agenda, and home-work on the board when students walk in. If you are not assigning homework for that night, put "No Homework" on the board so that students do not ask "Is there homework?" I cannot stress enough the importance of explaining the difference between a "due date" and a "deadline" for assignments. I label each homework assignment with a "DD" for due date and a "DL" for deadline. Be very clear with students and parents that the "due date" is the day that the assignment is due and will be graded for full credit. Then explain that the "deadline" for an assignment is the last day an assignment can be turned in for credit. Setting clear parameters for due dates and deadlines at the start of the year will help develop your winning system. I always recommend emphasizing the difference between a "due date" and a "deadline" as much as I can in the first month of school. Everything that I mentioned can be written on a chalkboard or typed in a document or presentation. I personally would recommend going digital so that you can email the information to any students that are absent. I would recommend making a template for a "one-pager" document so that you do not need to write it afresh each day (Figure 1.2).

Date: Tuesday, September 9, 2020

Do Now: Write down your homework and then start the warm up

Homework: Ancient Civilization Reading and Questions: DD - 9/11, DL: 9/18

Objective: SWBAT: describe the 8 themes of geography

Agenda: Warm Up -> Close Read -> 8 Themes of Geography Reading/Questions -> Interactive Exit Ticket

Figure 1.2 An example of a "one-pager" (A page that is displayed on the classroom board that contains the date, do now, homework, objective, and agenda for a class that students see when they walk into the classroom.)

I have found that having all of this information on the board each and every day leads to me being more organized, but also to students being more organized. Having all of this information visible each day also leads to consistency and structure. Having the objective posted and visible for students is important so that students know what skill or topic they will be able to complete by the end of the class. Having a "do now" on the board instructs students on what they should do as soon as they walk in. This can entail starting a warm-up, grabbing a computer, or any other pertinent information. In my classroom, students are expected to grab papers from the side table each day and then start their warm-up immediately. If you are a teacher who is mostly paper-based and not computer-based, having the routine of students picking up papers as soon as they walk in allows more time for instruction in class as you are not wasting time passing out papers. Disclosing your agenda to the class each day also keeps students informed on what they will be doing in class that period. Adding a section for homework is important for students to stay organized as well. At most schools, students have some sort of planner that they can write their homework assignments in. If you make writing down homework a routine from the first week of the year, you will have a higher percentage of students completing homework throughout the school year. Also, having a designated homework bin for students to turn in work adds another layer of structure for your class. When students are assigned homework, they should be expected to turn in their homework to the homework bin on the way into class. This allows for an easy way to collect homework assignments and again saves time collecting in papers.

Establishing Clear Rules and Expectations

The second step of creating a winning classroom system is establishing clear classroom rules and expectations while staying consistent in enforcing your rules and expectations throughout the entire school year. The first four days of the school year should focus on establishing classroom rules, routines, and culture. Learning the names of your students builds classroom culture and makes students feel valued. A strategy that I have always used is to have students put name tags on their desks during the first week of school. This assists me, and their peers, to learn everyone's names quickly. There can be up to five or six elementary schools feeding into a given middle school, which means that students might only know a few others in their class. There may be new students to your school if you teach seventh or eighth grade as well. Learning the names of your students helps with enforcing rules and expectations in the classroom. A student is going to have a better response when you address them by their name instead of throwing commands at them without using their name.

Going over your classroom rules and routines during the first week of school ensures students know exactly what you expect from the get-go. However, before going over classroom rules and expectations, be sure to introduce yourself and tell the class a little about you. You could start by showing a picture of you from the summer and listing your interests. I would then pass out a syllabus and begin going over classroom rules and expectations. Having the rules and routines written down in a syllabus helps students remember what you expect of them. Most teachers create their own syllabus. Below is an example of my syllabus that can serve as a template or guide in creating yours (Figures 1.3 and 1.4).

Most students in secondary school have five or six other teachers, all with their own rules and expectations. It can be hard for an eleven-year-old to remember all of the rules for several different teachers. I would advise not making more than five or six overarching classroom rules and making those rules clear and concise. I then would suggest having no more than three to four daily routines as well. I will give you my rules in the classroom as an example:

Rule 1: Please do not talk when the teacher is talking.

Rule 2: Respect yourself and your classmates (Golden Rule).

Rule 3: Take responsibility for your actions and words.

Rule 4: Please raise your hand to contribute to the class discussion.

Rule 5: Seats will change on a frequent basis; it does not mean you are in trouble if your seat moves!

I always make time to ask students if they have any questions, and then I start by discussing my classroom routines. Notice how I did not include rules such as "Show up to class on time" or "No cursing in the classroom." These are general school rules and students already know these expectations. School rules apply to every person, so I am not going to waste time going over them. Students should know the school's tardy policy, so I am not going to make that a classroom rule. At most schools, students are taught the tardy policy and other "school rules" in their homeroom class.

Contact Information

Mr. Stephen Katzel:
6th Grade Social Studies & Team Leader
Email: Stephen.x.katzel@XXXX@XXXX.org
School Phone: 301-XXX-XXXX

Course Overview

The Goal of Sixth Grade Social Studies is to enhance student's understanding of the ancient and modern worlds. The course is designed to develop academic skills through the lens of social studies education. Critical thinking skills will be taught throughout the school year. Students will have many chances to collaborate and interact with their peers when analyzing content.

Unit 1 – Ancient History through modern analysis: (6,000 BCE – 650 CE)
- Review & Overview – Themes of Geography
- The Beginnings of Civilizations
- Rise of Cities

Unit 2 – Classical History (500 CE – 1500 CE)
- Analysis of Citizenship
- Structures of governments
- Development of Advanced Technologies

Unit 3 – Modern History (1501 CE – Present)
- Globalization
- Impact of advanced technology

Unit 4 – Economics in the Modern World
- Macroeconomics
- Microeconomics

Classroom Norms

1. Put forth your best effort each class
2. Arrive to class before the bell rings
3. Arrive to class ready to learn
4. Follow the beginning of class procedures
5. No bathroom passes first/last 10 minutes of class
6. Take responsibility for the quality of your work

Suggested Materials

- Sharpened pencils
- Pens
- Wireless Mouse
- Paper
- Water Bottle

Figure 1.3 The first page of a classroom syllabus. (The first page of a syllabus that includes a teacher's contact information, course overview, classroom norms, and suggested class materials.)

Grading Policy
A -100%-89.5%
B - 89.4%-79.5%
C - 79.4% - 69.5%
D - 69.4%-59.5%
E - 59.4% & Below

GRADE CATEGORIES
60% - Formative Assessments
20%- Summative Assessments
10% - Homework
10% - 5 Paragraph Essay
     (Quarter 1 & 3 Only)
10% - Content Project
     (Quarter 2 & 4 Only)

LATE WORK
DUE DATE – day the assignment is due.
DEADLINE – last day to turn in work for credit.

Work turned in after the due date will lose 5%.
No work will be accepted after the deadline unless a student has excused absences.

Absences and Make-up work
- All necessary work must be completed while a student is absent or immediately upon return to school. Any assignments previously announced will be due on the day the student returns to school.
- All work missed because of an absence will be due no later than three school days after a student returns to school.
- Students are responsible to meet with the teacher to learn about missed work and missed instruction during study hall.
- Students are expected to know and makeup work from any absences over the year, both excused and unexcused.
- Students can access their missing work through the "Make-Up Binder" or by emailing the teacher for a digital copy.
- Students will be allowed one day for each day of an excused absence to make-up work.
- If an assignment is announced in class for a future date before a student is absent, the assignment will be given during study hall once the student returns to school.
- Work missed while a student is absent from class for reasons which are unexcused must be discussed with the teacher at study hall.

Figure 1.4 The second page of a classroom syllabus. (The second page of a syllabus that includes the teacher's grading policy, grade categories, late work policy, and absence policy.)

Rules Versus Routines

Classroom rules and classroom routines may seem similar, but they are different. Rules define what behavior is appropriate in the classroom for given situations, and routines give students specific steps to follow when performing certain actions. Classroom routines are important to establish as well. You may be wondering "When should I start going over routines with my classes?" You should go over routines with your classes during the first week of school so that students know what you expect from them from the start of the year. Throughout the first week of school, you should go over the routines with your classes each day and praise students for following your routines. The first daily routine I go over with students is to pick up all of the papers they need for class on the side table. Having this routine allows for students to have each paper they need for the day. This routine also saves instructional time, as you do not need to constantly pass out papers. The second daily routine I establish is that once students get to their seats after collecting their papers, they immediately write down their homework, even if it is "none." The third daily routine or "next step" I establish is that students quietly start their warm-up as soon as they finish writing down their homework. For my third routine to work, I need to provide a warm-up for students to complete on a daily basis. I make sure that the warm-up aides in my hook (way to grab students' interest for the lesson) so that students are excited and interested in the day's learning. I typically allocate five minutes to complete the warm-up and limit the activity to two to three questions about a writing passage or picture that is relevant to my instruction.

Finding Your Own Teaching Style

A new teacher may or may not know what their own "style" of teaching is their first day of school. Before the first week of school, I challenge all new teachers to write a paragraph describing their style of classroom management during their student teaching experience. I then ask the new teacher to list what about their own "teaching style" is important to them or makes them proud. Are they a strong lecturer? Are they good at providing materials? Are they good at making real-world connections to content? There are a lot of ways new teachers can analyze themselves and it is important that, as a new educator, you come to your own realization of what your style is. This can be done through trial and error. Your style could even change mid-year if you want to shake things up. I personally try to make my classroom rules and routines unique to my teaching style and management philosophy. Again, I would suggest not having your classroom rules overlap with school rules. The rules in your district or school's code of conduct do not need to be reiterated. For example, students hopefully already know that cell phones are not allowed during class time; hence, you do not need to mention "no cell phones" in your core classroom rules. I cannot stress strongly enough having your classroom rules and routines written down in the syllabus. I would also recommend sending an electronic copy of your syllabus home to all of your students' parents and guardians as well. A classroom syllabus is usually the outline of a course of study, so I would include the topics that you are covering in class each quarter as well. It does not need to be very long, but it is important for students and parents to know what they will be studying in your class that year. I would also suggest putting your school email address on the syllabus.

Establishing rules and procedures helps you build a winning system in your classroom. Having the rules and routines written down in addition to going over them the first week of school is important. Consistently enforcing your classroom rules and sticking with your routines throughout the entire year will pay dividends. Students should know exactly what is expected of them as soon as they walk into your classroom. Unpredictability leads to higher rates of students misbehaving and leads to more behavior management issues. A huge mistake I have seen newly qualified teachers make is having each class period brainstorm with the teacher what the classroom rules should be. Don't do this! Your rules and routines should be consistent across all of your classes, which will make enforcing and remembering the rules easier for you and your students. Also, class schedules change frequently throughout the first month of school. If one of your student's switches class periods, they would have to learn a whole new set of rules if you let each class make their own rules.

Classroom Mission Statements

Having a classroom mission statement also aids in establishing your winning system. The statement can be made into a poster and hung up in your room so that your students know what the purpose of your class is. I would start your mission statement with this beginning: "Mr. Katzel's classroom mission is to…" Each teacher's mission statement will be different but should have common themes. Building capacity, skills, personal success, and knowledge are key themes of a mission statement. When students see that you have made a goal for yourself as an educator, they will know that you are not just coming in for your paycheck each day and that you care about their success in your classroom and beyond. When students know that you genuinely care about their success, they will be more willing to take risks in their learning and be an active participant in your room.

Final Thoughts

This may all seem overwhelming as a first-year teacher, but following these steps will help you develop systems to make you less stressed as the year goes on! Remember the saying: "Rome was not built in a day." It is going to take a week or so for your students to remember all of your rules and routines. However, once they get the hang of it you will see that your classroom is running like a well-oiled machine. Students will know exactly what is expected of them when they walk in and when they walk out. Make sure you stay consistent, and do not be afraid to remind students of your rules. Some say your first year of teaching is your worst year. I do not agree with that: your mindset and preparation dictate the outcome of your first year. Make your first year of teaching your best year. Having a winning system in place will help you with this!

2

Long-Term and Short-Term Planning

Short-term planning is more effective after developing a long-term plan for the quarter. Both long-term and short-term planning serve as blueprints for how you teach your content on a daily basis. Long-term planning and short-term planning are entirely different concepts. Long-term planning involves having a collection of topics that you know you will cover in the near future. Typically, using a calendar for the quarter and putting a topic of study for each date is the "standard" for long-term planning. If other teachers are teaching the same content as you, I recommend long-term planning with them so that you are on the same page in terms what should be taught and for how long each topic should be covered. You must be wondering, "how do I figure out which topics to fill in for which dates?" The easy answer is to look at your district's curriculum and decide with your cohort (other teachers that teach the same subject as you) how many days certain topics will take, which topics to spend more time on, which dates you will use for quizzes or tests, which dates you will assign homework, and which dates you will distribute study guides for the tests and quizzes. Writing out these categories on a planning calendar may seem cumbersome, and it is difficult the first time you do it. But completing the quarterly planning calendar in this much detail will save you significant time down the road in your planning. Having a detailed long-term plan will ideally help you and your grade-level cohort realize what you actually want students to know by certain dates and prioritize which topics are most important.

If you are unlucky and have to plan by yourself, or have a cohort that does not team plan, do not worry! I advise teachers to start their calendar by numbering each date and then figure out how many days you have to teach for the quarter. Below is an example of a quarterly planning calendar (Figures 2.1 and 2.2).

	Sunday	Monday	Tuesday	Wednesday	Thursday	Friday	Saturday
Unit 2- Week #1	11/8	11/9 1 Citizenship in Ancient Times!	11/10 2 Citizenship in Ancient Times!	11/11 3 (Half Day) Purpose of Ancient Governments	11/12 4 Secondary Source Analysis	11/13 5 Purpose of Government (Secondary Source Analysis) HW #1	11/14
Unit 2- Week #2	11/15	11/16 6 Traits of Citizenship	11/17 7 Mapping Ancient Middle East	11/18 8 Ancient Civilizations	11/19 9 Map Quiz	11/20 10 (Half Day) Picture Analysis	11/21
Unit 2- Week #3	11/22	11/23 11 Warring City States	11/24 12 Primary Source Analysis HW #2	*11/25* *No School (Thanksgiving Break)*	*11/26* *No School (Thanksgiving Break)*	*11/27* *No School (Thanksgiving Break)*	11/28
Unit 2- Week #4	11/29	11/30 13 Class Discussion: Choose a side in Ancient Times!	12/1 14 Class Discussion: Choose a side in Ancient Times!	12/2 15 Claim and Evidence Practice	12/3 16 Claim and Evidence Practice HW #3	12/4 17 Historical Essay Prep	12/5
Unit 2- Week #5	12/6	12/7 Science Education Field Trip (Entire 6th Grade)	12/8 Science Education Field Trip (Entire 6th Grade)	12/9 Science Education Field Trip (Entire 6th Grade)	12/10 Science Education Field Trip (Entire 6th Grade)	12/11 Science Education Field Trip (Entire 6th Grade)	12/12
Unit 2- Week #6	12/13	12/14 18 Historical Essay	12/15 19 Historical Essay	12/16 20 Historical Essay	12/17 21 Historical Essay	12/18 22 Historical Essay	12/19

Figure 2.1 The first six weeks of a long-term planning calendar. (A diagram showing the first six weeks of a long-term planning calendar that includes each date being numbered sequentially, days a teacher will assign homework, and the dates of exams.)

Winter Break	12/20	12/21	12/22	12/23	12/24	12/25	12/26
	Winter Break (No School)	Winter Break (No School)	Winter Break (No School)	Winter Break (No School)	Winter Break (No School)	Winter Break (No School)	
Winter Break	12/27	12/28	12/29	12/30	12/31	1/1	1/2
	Winter Break (No School)	Winter Break (No School)	Winter Break (No School)	Winter Break (No School)	Winter Break (No School)	Winter Break (No School)	
Unit 2- Week #7	1/3	1/4 23 Inventions of the Ancient World	1/5 24 Impact of Technology HW #4	1/6 25 Social Class Analysis	1/7 26 Social Class Analysis	1/8 27 Impact of War	1/9
Unit 2- Week #8	1/10	1/11 28 Class Discussion: Art Analysis	1/12 29 Class Discussion: Art Analysis	1/13 30 Thesis Statement	1/14 31 Paragraph Activity- Thesis Statement Practice	1/15 32 Start of Rebellions	1/16
Unit 2- Week #9	1/17	1/18 No School (MLK Day)	1/19 33 Impact of Rebellions	1/20 34 Review Day	1/21 35 Test	1/22 36 Review Common Errors on Test	1/23
Unit 2- Week #10	1/24	1/25 37 Webquest	1/26 38 Webquest	1/27 39 Article Analysis	1/28 40 Article Analysis	1/29 41 (Half Day) Newspaper Article	1/30

Figure 2.2 The last four weeks of a long-term planning calendar. (A diagram showing the last four weeks of a long-term planning calendar that includes each date being numbered sequentially, days a teacher will assign homework, and the dates of exams.)

Although most school districts use the "quarter" system, some quarters may be longer or shorter than others due to the structure of the calendar or school/district events. For example, in certain school districts in the Washington, DC, area, sixth-grade students have a two-and-a-half-day overnight field trip in the fall or winter each school year. Because there is usually a high number of students, districts have to break up the trip into two sessions, which means that the trip covers five days of quarter two each year. Students have activities at school while their peers are on the trip, but they do

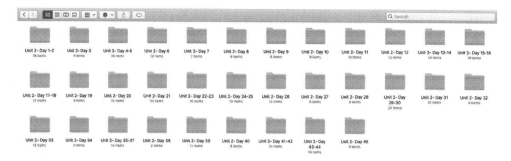

Figure 2.3 Folders that contain lesson plans and resources for a unit of study. (Forty-five folders that are labeled sequentially and contain all lesson plans, worksheets, and needed materials for an entire unit of planning.)

not see their normal teachers. This means that I have five fewer days of instruction in quarter two. Since I long-term plan, I can provision for this. Maybe I could give a bit more homework during this quarter than I typically would, due to not having as many days of instruction. Or I could assign a project to be completed at home instead of giving class time for that subject matter or topic. There are numerous ways I could approach the issue of having fewer instructional days, and long-term planning makes it easier for me to address this. Another benefit of long-term planning is that it allows a team of two or more cohort members to have a shared vision on what instruction will look like for the quarter in their respective subject. In my long-term planning calendar, I purposely label each day so that I can stay better organized when I am making lesson plans. The numbering allows for me to align my long-term planning with my folders containing the lesson's materials: note in Figure 2.3 how easy it is for me to match my lesson plan with the folder that contains all of my materials (Figure 2.3).

Listing the topic of study for each date of the long-term planning calendar assists the teacher to stay more organized. It is easier to track the flow of the unit when you put the topic on the date as well. Labeling which dates have homework increases a teacher's organization and serves as an extra reminder to pass out the homework. Having teachers share their course calendars can help parents stay in the loop with their child's education and allows for the teacher to become more transparent. This will also allow for parents to be "in the know" about what is occurring in your classroom. The course calendar can be a simplified version of your quarterly long-term plan for the unit. Noting which topic will be covered on each date will allow parents and students to know exactly what will be covered each day of the unit. I would recommend sending a paper copy of the calendar home with each student or emailing it to all of the parents.

You should never feel that your subject matter is a "secret." Parents will be appreciative that you sent a class calendar home, and it reflects well on you as a teacher. If your school district has an online portal where you can easily post the class calendar, adding it there would be fine as well.

Using Your Blueprint to Plan Individual Lessons

Long-term planning provides a blueprint of what to teach and for how long each subject will be taught. The first thing to do before you begin short-term planning is to read the curriculum guide that your school or district has (hopefully) provided for you. While reading the curriculum guide, you should annotate the guide and consider the following questions: "What lessons do I like and find engaging? Which lessons are not good at all? What lessons could I modify to enhance student achievement?" The curriculum guide for your subject matter should ideally include mid-point quizzes or other formative assessments and summative assessments. Your short-term planning ideology should also include covering the topics on exams. I would never recommend teaching to a quiz or a test, but it is important to cover the topics laid out in curriculum guide. Keeping all of this in mind, you are now ready to start planning individual lessons.

Depending on your school's schedule, you will have between forty to sixty minutes of instructional time for each class you teach. Your goal is to utilize every minute of instructional time. Each lesson plan should have a structure so that the lesson has a clear beginning, middle, and end. The start of each lesson should have a "hook" or attention grabber for students. The warm-up should not take more than ten minutes. I would recommend making most warm-ups or activators no more than five minutes long. It may seem tedious to have a warm-up for each class period, but this helps get students interested in your lesson and adds structure to your classroom. I typically make my warm-up an introduction to the topic of the day. I try to make it as interesting as possible so that students are intrigued about what they are learning that day. I typically spend two to three minutes per class period going over the warm-up and answering any questions that students may have. I would suggest having no more than four questions included in your warm-up. I allocate different amounts of time for the middle of my lesson depending on the topic I am covering and how I want to assess student learning through the exit ticket. I typically make the middle of my lesson last between twenty to thirty minutes. In the middle part of my lesson, I make sure to have a clear "I do," "We do," and a "You do." Even if I allow students to work on the assignment with partners for that class period, I ensure that I retain this structure. For example, I am teaching my class about how to make a claim and support that claim with evidence. I would model/review with the class how to make a claim and support the claim with evidence. I would then complete the task so that the class has a clear model of how to answer the question. I would then go over a second example with the class and call on students to help me answer the questions. After this, I would have students complete the assignment. Some teachers use the assignment they give in class as a benchmark or check for whether the class understands the topic. I personally recommend giving an "exit ticket" or assignment that summarizes the learning for the day. Essentially, an exit ticket is a formative assessment to check on the progress of your students. This allows the teacher to see what students understand and what they do not understand, which ultimately guides the planning of the teacher. The "end" of the lesson typically takes five to ten minutes. Regardless of how you structure the class period, it is important to collect classwork at the end of the class period. I know thinking about all of this during planning may seem cumbersome; however, your students will benefit from your organization. Using a curriculum guide to devise warm-ups, worksheets, and exit tickets would make planning immensely easier. The first year I plan lessons for a new curriculum is always the hardest. But since I am so diligent in how I plan, I do not stress in the years after since I have already put in the hard work. The next few paragraphs will explain the steps to take after designing the structure of your lessons.

Lesson Plan Formats

Each lesson plan is unique, but how you write out the lesson plan should be standardized to your own personal preferences. Some schools ask teachers to submit their lesson plans, while other schools are more hands-off and do not ask for copies of lesson plans. Also, the amount of detail each person wants to put into the lesson plan can vary. I personally view each lesson plan as a blueprint for what I am going to cover for the day. I include important information to guide my teaching for that day. However, I never write a script for what I am going to say in the lesson, as I do not believe that "scripting" is effective. In fact, it is an antiquated practice. I do not have a particular article to prove that "scripting is ineffective." However, I have observed scripted lessons and they felt forced and awkward. You can plan for potential questions, but students might ask a question that was not "provisioned" in the script, which derails the entire concept of "scripting." Some teachers like having a script to work from, but I feel it makes the delivery of the lesson forced and hurts the flow of the class. Regardless of what your school expects of you in terms of lesson plans, it is important to make a lesson plan for each and every day of the school year. Yes, you read that correctly: you should have a lesson plan for each and every day of the school year, and it should include an objective, standards, agenda, time estimations on the agenda, vocabulary, and essential questions for the day. I include more information, but the information listed here should be the bare minimum. I include an example of a lesson plan I made below (see Figure 2.4). I know that my lesson plan is not as detailed as it could be, but it includes all of the important information that I need to successfully teach that day. I highly recommend reviewing your lesson plan the night before each class or in the morning before students come into school. You should never feel like you are "winging it." In Figure 2.4, you will find an example of the lesson plan template that I use for my own planning. It is concise and easy to follow. I want to explain my rationale for how/why I structure my lesson plans the way I do. Your school district may ask for different things to be part of your lesson plan, or not ask for a plan at all. I include the "basics" of objective, standards, and essential questions because, in my opinion, all lesson plans should incorporate these aspects. I always include the unit and day of the unit, so that the individual lesson plan matches with my long-term planning sheet and folders on my computer. Also, I include prior learning so that it is clear to whoever is reading my plan that this lesson builds on previously learned material and gives the teacher background to the context of my lesson. I include academic vocabulary so that the teacher knows what words will need to be defined and discussed during the lesson. This also allows the teacher to be reminded of what words will be new or challenging to students. I include the state standards to show that the lesson I planned aligns with state standards and the curriculum. If your lesson does not align with the curriculum, then your supervisor may query the relevance of the lesson. I include the daily objective in the lesson plan to make it clear what I hope to accomplish by teaching this lesson. The essential questions are included so that the teacher knows the key themes that are driving the lesson. I always include what the warm-up is so that the teacher knows how the class will start and how the learning will be framed for that particular lesson. The exit ticket/summarizer is included in the lesson plan so that the teacher knows how the lesson will wrap up and will be able to measure how much the class learned from that particular lesson. The timing of the lesson is extremely important to include, because the teacher needs to be able to pace themselves throughout the lesson and have an idea of how long each activity should take. This allows the teacher to have a plan for the pacing of the lesson and allows the teacher of the lesson plan to know how long each activity will take. Figure 2.4 provides an example of an individualized lesson plan (Figure 2.4).

Sample Lesson Plan: 6th Grade Social Studies

Teacher: Mr. Katzel	Grade/Subject: 6th Grade Social Studies	Unit/Day of Unit: Unit 1, Day 2
Periods: 1, 2, 6, 7	Previous Learning: 1. Analyzed maps of Europe 2. Analyzed the impact of geography on civilizations	State Standard(s): GEO159- Describe human and physical characteristics of geography by analyzing maps and other secondary sources
Academic Vocabulary: Human Geography, Physical Geography, Human Characteristics, Physical Characteristics	Daily Objective (In Student Friendly Language): SWBAT (Students will be able to) identify human and physical characteristics by analyzing maps and other secondary sources	Essential Question: Why do maps change?
Warm Up/Introduction: "Analyze a Map" Worksheet	Exit Ticket/Summarization: On the classroom portal, there will be multiple choice questions on geography.	Lesson Timing (Estimation in Minutes): 1. Warm Up (5) 2. Geography Close Read (10) 3. Map Analysis (15) 4. Secondary Source Analysis (15) 5. Review "Secondary Source Analysis" (5) 6. Exit Ticket on Geography (10)

Figure 2.4 Sample Lesson Plan: Sixth Grade Social Studies. (A sample lesson plan for a sixth-grade social studies class. The lesson plan includes the objective, state standards, agenda, time estimation for agenda items, academic vocabulary, essential question, teacher' name, and class periods.)

Adding Time Estimates

One detail of the lesson plan that often gets overlooked is adding time estimations to each lesson plan. It is a tough balance to not over-plan or under-plan a lesson. If you do not plan enough things to do, you will not cover the entirety of the class period. But if you plan too many things to do, you will not get through everything! The advice I always give first-year teachers is to add a time estimation for each activity so that you do not under- or over-plan a lesson. Estimating how long an activity will take can be difficult. I recommend completing the activity yourself so that you can gauge roughly how long it will take students. Each person may have different estimates for assignments depending on their students' abilities. If there is ever a time where you have not planned enough activities, you can have students interact constructively. What I mean by that is to give students time to talk about what they learned. For example, after giving students an exit ticket, I may realize I still have 8 minutes left in class. So, I would tell the class, "Please take the next 4 minutes and find a person in the class to discuss the exit ticket with. After the 4 minutes are up, I will randomly call on groups to help me answer the questions." If you do not want to have students discuss the exit ticket, you can have students discuss a classwork assignment instead. If you do not want to have students discuss assignments, you could always pull up an educational video that relates to the topic.

Aligning to Your Objectives

Another tip I give to first-year teachers is to ensure that the lesson you are teaching aligns with the learning objective you wrote for the day. The learning objective itself should always start with the acronym SWBAT, which stands for "Students Will Be Able To." I start each class period by reading the objective to the class so they know what they will accomplish in that class period. This adds a sense of purpose to the learning and another layer of structure to your classroom. Remember, the more structured your classroom is, the better off you will be.

Numbering Your Plans

Numbering each lesson plan by the unit and day of the unit will assist you in being more organized. I did not start numbering my lesson plans until my second year of teaching – I wish that somebody told me to do this in my first year! I could have saved so much time in my first year of teaching if I went back to edit and modify the lessons from my first year. Although it will take you some time to make a lesson plan for each day, it will help you develop as a teacher and as a planner. If a supervisor asks to see a lesson plan, you will be able to produce it with ease.

Final Thoughts

Being extremely organized in your long-term and short-term planning positively affects other aspects of your job and daily routine. Each day, before school starts, you will be able to easily locate your presentation, lesson plan, and resources in one centralized location. It takes me no more than five minutes to pull up all of my resources on my computer and to set up my classroom for the day. Numbering and organizing your lesson plans and materials allows for you to stay organized more efficiently. Having hundreds of files in one folder leads to materials being all over the place and difficult to access. Being able to locate lesson plans and materials with ease saves a lot of time and heartache. I have seen first-year teachers scrambling to locate all of their files in the morning because they did not have a system in place to organize their materials. By implementing a well-organized long-term and short-term planning system, you will be well on your way to having a winning system and easier mornings! Also, if you ever need to call a substitute teacher, having all of your lesson plans organized helps make your life easier. You can share any lesson plan and materials with a substitute teacher with relative ease since everything is in one centralized location. I have seen a lot of first-year teachers not be able to find materials or lesson plans that they created because they did not have an organized system for their planning. Remember, having a standardized lesson plan each day allows for you to have a blueprint to refer to before the start of each school day. You will know exactly what state standard you are teaching, what activities you are implementing, and you will have an estimation on how long each activity will take. You will head into your first class of the day well organized and ready to deliver a high-quality lesson as a direct result of your winning system.

3

Use Technology, It Is Your Friend

Organizing Lesson Plans

Using technology efficiently will make teaching easier due to the amount of time you will save in your daily activities at work. Since the previous chapter was on short-term and long-term planning, I will first discuss how technology can make your planning more efficient and easier to manage. Whether you are more comfortable using your own personal computer or using a cloud service, it is important to have an organizational system where you store your lesson plans. The purpose of saving your files is that it will save you time each school year when you are looking at your lesson plans. For each lesson plan I make, I create a folder. The organizational system I recommend is pretty simple. I always have a "main" folder that I name after the unit of study. For example, "Unit 1 – World War I." I will then make a folder for each lesson that falls under the first unit of study. For example, my first lesson of the unit's folder's name will be "Unit 1 – Day 1." I will keep all of the files for that lesson in that folder: the lesson plan, the presentation, and any worksheets or materials for the lesson. Whether it is a word document or a PDF, I make sure to have all of the resources in one folder. This helps me stay organized and able to easily access any lessons in an instant. The following lesson will also have a folder; I would name this "Unit 1 – Day 2." Having this system of organization allows me to be a more efficient teacher and planner because I know where I will put the lesson plans, emails, files, grades, calendars, and all other related items. This also helps when a student misses class.

If I know that a student will be absent on a specific date, I can easily email the assignments to their parents because I have everything digitally and readily available. If you have a paper copy of a great worksheet or lesson plan, scan it! Having everything available online eliminates the need to keep papers. I know it may seem cumbersome to take the time to have individual folders for each lesson; however, you will thank yourself the following year since all of your work will be readily accessible when you start to plan for the new school year. You will have a folder covering the entire school year, and will be able to access files, lesson plans, and presentations with ease. When I help first-year teachers with planning, I am able to give them lessons for every day of the year as a direct result of my organizational system. I also keep my long-term planning calendar in the "main" unit folder as well. I have four main folders for the year that represent the four units or quarters for the year. The names of my other three folders are "Unit 2 – World War II," "Unit 3 – The Cold War," and "Unit 4 – Post Cold War." Within each of those folders, you would find the same organizational system as the folder for my first unit. This allows me to have a centralized location for my long-term plans and daily lesson plans.

Tips for Finding Good Lessons Online

You will not always get all of the lesson plans you need from your district's curriculum, and looking online for supporting materials is acceptable. To add to how technology helps with planning, it is also important to know what to look for when you are searching for materials online. If you are searching for a specific topic or material, type in the topic and add "doc" or "PDF" to the search. Doing this will help you find a lot more resources than just typing the topic's name into a search bar. I have found resources online that are relevant to my instruction, but I always make sure I edit the content of them to fit my own style of teaching and the needs of my students. If you find an assignment that is a "doc" it will be easy for you to edit. Editing a document that is a "PDF" may seem much more challenging; however, if you type "PDF to DOC converter" into any search engine, there are multiple websites that are out there that allow you to convert a PDF into an editable document for free. If you want to make a scanned PDF document into a word document that you can edit, look up "OCR converter" in a search engine. There are a bunch of free OCR converters that can used to convert scanned PDF files into Word files. Before I realized I could convert PDF documents, I was always very disappointed that I could not edit PDFs that could be useful for my classroom. Now I regularly edit PDF documents to meet the needs of my students, and the results have been wonderful. I never discourage anyone from looking online for supporting materials for their classroom, but I do caution new teachers against just using someone else's worksheets or ideas without editing them to fit their own students' needs. It is imperative new teachers (or anyone using online resources) edit them to meet the needs of their students. I also would recommend converting all of your PDF documents to an editable format. This allows you to email work to students that may have broken a finger or arm and can't write but can type for a period of time. Also, having every file as a "doc" and "PDF" allows you to edit assignments in the future in case the curriculum changes.

Incorporating Videos

Regardless of the subject or topic that you are covering in class, it is important to include videos in your instruction. I am not an advocate of using videos in instruction every day, but it is important to use videos as an instruction aid. I show approximately one video a week, of not more than ten minutes long. Using a variety of internet sites for videos will benefit your instruction. Showing videos with a specific purpose in your classroom will help students feel more engaged. If you decide to show a video that is more than five minutes and just expect students to watch it, chances are a good chunk of students will not be engaged. During the video, have students fill out a worksheet that prompts them to analyze what they are watching. For example, I showed a video that re-enacts a historical event that was relevant to my instruction. While students were watching the video, I had them answer questions that they only could correctly respond to by paying attention. Having this assignment during the video helped ensure that they were paying attention and that the video I was showing had an academic purpose.

Using Technology for Grading

Technology also helps you keep up with the demanding task of grading assignments. Most districts expect teachers to input at least one grade per week, regardless of the subject matter. I agree that each teacher should put in at least one grade a week. This allows students to see how they are progressing in the class, and also allows teachers to track the progress of students. Regardless of the subject that you teach, you can use technology to help you with grading. Depending on your school district, there are plenty of online tools to automatically grade multiple-choice assignments. Many districts have popular programs that allow teachers to post assignments, quizzes, multiple-choice assignments, and a class calendar, and to email parents, through their class page. I strongly believe that assessments should not be limited to multiple-choice questions; however, teachers can integrate an exit ticket or short quiz that strictly has only multiple-choice questions once in a while. Too many first-year teachers get bogged down in grading and then get overwhelmed with the number of assignments they need to grade. It is impossible to grade each assignment and then put it into the gradebook, all while maintaining a life–work balance. Learn your school district's grading policy so that you know how many assignments need to be entered each month. If you have to assign classwork and not grade it, so be it.

Tools to Help You Meet Different Learning Needs

Regardless of where you teach, you will encounter diverse learning needs, and technology can help you meet those needs. Some students struggle with long texts and reading comprehension. Earlier, when I suggested that you have every document you use in class in your own folders, there was another reason for this: having everything digitally available can help students that struggle with reading through the use of technology. There are plenty of online programs that read highlighted texts or entire pages of information to students. If a student struggles with reading, you can either email them the reading or post it to your "online classroom." Once students open the document, they can use various programs that will read the text to them. Having roughly five to ten pairs of headphones available for students is important for this as well, so that the rest of the class does not hear the computer reading the text to the students. I have found that allowing students to use "read to" technology has boosted the grades of the students that need the most help with reading and reading comprehension. I realize that not every teacher is lucky enough to have a one-to-one ratio of laptops to students, but if you have laptops for students, keeping this in mind will help your students. This also saves time from you or your paraeducator reading each assignment or reading to students every class period.

Online Quizzes for Self-Assessments

Another way to incorporate technology into your classroom is to use online "quiz websites," where students can make a username and participate in an interactive quiz. Most such sites award students points for answering correct questions, and award additional points depending on how quickly they answer the question. I definitely would not recommend using these "fun" quiz websites as the basis for an actual grade. Rather, use them as an informal way for students to self-assess their own progress. There are multiple websites that let you create or use premade quizzes with your class. Students can typically answer the quiz questions by using a laptop or a cell phone. If your school has laptops that are accessible to students, I would suggest not allowing students use their cellphones to participate in the quiz game. The use of "online quiz websites" helps make your class feel interactive and engaging to students. Using this tool in your classroom allows you to integrate technology into your lesson plans, makes the learning fun, and can act as an informal "exit ticket."

Final Thoughts

Efficient use of technology will allow you to implement a winning system with greater ease. Ensuring that your lesson plans are easily accessible is crucial throughout your first year of teaching. I recommend having all of your lesson plans stored in two separate places to be safe. There are many "cloud" companies that charge reasonable prices to store your files online. Many school districts pay for such facilities so that their teachers can back up their files for free. If you have this luxury, definitely take advantage of it! Clearly labeling your lesson plans by the unit and day will allow you to access the materials with ease. The search for supplemental materials online can lead to headaches. However, by tweaking your searches to include "doc" or "PDF," you will find a wealth of resources for free. Online websites that convert PDFs to text docs will allow you to differentiate your lesson plans to best meet the needs of your students. Incorporating videos into your instruction allows for students to visualize certain topics and ideas. However, being intentional in what you show, and for how long, determines the effectiveness what you show. Using technology to help you with grading is part of having a winning system. Incorporating an online quiz once or twice a semester helps in alleviating the pressure of grading. Researching online tools to help struggling readers in your class will pay dividends. Since you have a winning system in place, you will be able to share documents with students that require technology to read the contents of the assignments to them. Remember, make technology work for you, do not work for technology! Implementing a winning system will ensure that technology will always work for you.

4

Communication Is Key

Communicating effectively in all aspects of your job is important to winning your first year of teaching. Communicating effectively with bosses, colleagues, students, and parents help make your job easier.

What's Your Email Plan?

Making a plan for how you construct, organize, and respond to emails is the first step in communicating effectively. Depending on your school district, you might have two district email addresses. Many school districts partner with two different email providers. Usually, one is the "typical" work one and the other is more "up to speed" with cloud servicing and other modern features. School districts like to give teachers two email addresses so that we have options in terms of what we use. In the past, I wasted time each day checking both school-provided email addresses. To avoid checking two different email addresses, I started forwarding all of my emails to one email account. I found the instructions on how to forward the emails by conducting an online search for "how to forward all emails to one account" in a search engine. This process took five minutes to figure out and helped me stay more organized. Now I only have to check one email account and I spend less time searching for emails. A benefit of using an email with cloud storage is that when someone emails you, the email is never automatically deleted.

Creating Contact Lists

Having "contact lists" in your work email account enables you to communicate more efficiently with parents. After the first few weeks of school, I compile a list of students who may need extra support and additional parent check-ins. Extra support includes those struggling with work completion or turning in homework, or who need extra reminders to complete work from their parents. After compiling my list of students, I add the email addresses of their parents or guardians to a specified contact list in my email account named "Parent Check-Ins." I always make sure to BCC all emails I send to my "Parent Check-In" group. Using the "BCC" ("blind carbon copy") feature on your email hides the email addresses of all of the other people on the contact list, which gives them anonymity and privacy. I send study guides, class notes, answer keys, homework assignments, or just an email giving parents a heads up about big projects or assignments coming up in class. This allows parents of struggling students to know what is going on in my class, so they can further support those students at home. I try to send as many answer keys as I possibly can so that parents can support their student at home without having to do hours of research themselves. I have also noticed that the grades of struggling students have improved as a direct result of their parents providing extra support at home. Along with their grades improving, another benefit of having a "Parent Check-In" contact list is that parents know you are invested in their child's education and appreciate you contacting them throughout the school year. I know many teachers may counter this idea with a flawed statement such as "Students need to learn themselves without their parents checking in with them." However, I believe in building the capacity of my students while enlisting parental support at home. We see students for such a small portion of the day, having their parents on board and informed about your class can only help your students grow academically. I also recommend keeping a digital copy of the notes that you take in class, as this will allow you to have them readily available to send to parents.

Regular Parent Communications

Along with communicating with parents of students who need extra help, staying in contact with parents in general is beneficial. Sending a weekly or monthly email to all parents helps them to stayed informed. A short email including any major assignments or topics of study in the month helps parents know what is going on in your classroom. I also suggest sending home at least two positive emails to parents each week. The email does not need to be an essay; you can simply write two or three sentences. You can talk about a student giving a great project presentation, or something as simple as that they are "doing a great job participating." Often, the parents of our "high-achieving" students never receive any feedback from their child's teachers. Sending a positive email home allows for the parents of "high-achieving" students to feel that their child is being recognized and that their hard work is appreciated. Whenever you communicate with parents, it is important to keep a "communication log." Many school districts have their own computer program or website that acts as a "communication log." A communication log is a way for teachers to document any parent communication or classroom concerns with a student. When meeting with a parent about a concern, I make sure to check the communication log. In the communication log, you can put something as simple as "Spoke to John Doe about running in the hallway on 12/10." This would allow for you to easily document if a student is constantly running in the hallway and not changing their behavior. When calling the parent, you can say "On 12/10 I spoke to your son about running in the hallway. Today is 12/15, and I saw him running again. Can you please talk to your child about running in the hallway?" Documenting behavior this way will make your communication with parents clearer and allow you to be more organized. If your school district does not have a communication log, you can create your own document to keep track of students' behavior.

Preparing for Parent Conferences

Most school districts have at least one round of parent conferences, with some school districts having fall and spring parent conferences. Most school districts also have a "Back to School Night." I will talk about "Back to School Night" in the next paragraph. Knowing how to communicate with parents beforehand, and tactfully framing your ideas and talking points, are essential to a successful parent conference. For example, if I told a parent "your child is constantly disruptive and calls out in class," that sounds like I am being critical of the child and this could make the parent defensive, which could ultimately lead to a contentious conversation. However, if I said, "Your student sometimes struggles with raising his hand. Let's go over some strategies to help him with this," the way I framed my statement enlists the parent in helping me work with their child to build a collaborative relationship between the classroom and at home, with you and the parent. I would also

Teacher: Mr. Katzel, 6th Grade Team Leader & Social Studies	Email: step hen.X.XXX XXX@_____ __.com	School Phone: 209-XXX-XXXX	Student Name: John Doe	Q1 Grade: 92% (A) Formative Grade Percentage- 90% Summative Grade Percentage – 95% Homework Grade Percentage- 100% Essay Grade Percentage- 90%
Strengths 1. Asks for help/clarification 2. Comes to class on time 3. Comes prepared with materials	Area(s) to Discuss 1. Turning in homework on time	Action Steps for Success 1. Weekly check in from Mr. Katzel by email 2. Check assignments on the online portal	Action Steps for Success 3. Write down the homework each day in the student planner	Notes:

Figure 4.1 Sample resource that can be used for a parent–teacher conference. (A sample resource that contains the teacher's name, student's grade broken down by grading category, the strengths of a student, areas to discuss, action steps, and notes.)

recommend going to the parent conference with a checklist to go over. Remember, you set the tone for the parent conference! How you phrase your comments impacts the tone of the conference. At the end of the day, parents typically want what is best for their child and want to work with you to help their child succeed. Always remember that parent conferences are a tool to improve the student, not a session where you list complaints about a student. Figure 4.1 provides an example of a checklist that I have used in the past few years (Figure 4.1).

Back to School Night

"Back to School Night" is a great opportunity to introduce yourself to the school community and to the parents of your students. Most schools allocate five to ten minutes for each class period parent to come into your room. Make sure you speak loudly when parents come in and clean your classroom before the event. I always have copies of my syllabus readily available for parents on Back to School Night as well. I would advise making a presentation that introduces yourself; goes over your syllabus, your background in teaching, and what subjects you will cover for the year; and explains what classroom procedures that

Welcome to Back to School Night!

Greetings Parents and Guardians! My name is Mr. Katzel and I will be
your student's Social Studies teacher for the 20XX-20XX school year!
This will be my 8th year teaching and I am looking forward to
working with you!

Figure 4.2 A one-pager that can be shown for Back to School Night. (A one-pager that contains a picture of a teacher along with a message welcoming parents and guardians to Back to School Night. The image contains the amount of years the teacher has taught.)

you have in place. At the end of the day, parents want to see that you care about your job and that you care about the school. Leaving the last minute open for questions is always a good idea so that parents can ask you anything they might be curious about. I wouldn't allow more than a minute for questions, otherwise you will not have enough time to cover everything! Figure 4.2 provides an example of the first page of my presentation I show to parents during "Back to School Night." Having a "welcome" slide shows parents your background and a little bit about yourself. It is also very important to include the phrase "Parents and Guardians." Some students are being raised by a guardian, and I always want everyone feel welcome and included. In the second part of the presentation, I go over the entire syllabus with parents so they know what to expect from my class for the year. In the third part of my presentation, I show parents an example of the "one-pager" that students see each day when they walk in. This allows parents to see that the objective, homework, date, and agenda are posted every day. In the last part of the presentation I go over the yearly goals that I hope to accomplish with my students outside of the content. My yearly goals for my sixth-grade students are: goal setting, developing study skills, and learning time management. Depending on your grade level and subject, your goals may be different (Figure 4.2).

Managing All Those Emails

Responding to work emails in a timely manner is extremely important. If you receive an email that requires a direct response from you, answer that email within one business day. Not responding to emails in a timely manner will not reflect well on you. As an educator, you may receive dozens of emails each day and feel overwhelmed by them. That is why it is important to allocate at least fifteen to twenty minutes each day to respond to emails. I do not suggest answering emails once you get home from work or on weekends unless you deem it absolutely necessary. In my first few years of teaching, I found myself constantly answering emails in the evening and on weekends. I felt overwhelmed by this and felt that I was always in a "work" mindset. Now, I tell my students at the start of the year that emails received after five pm will receive a response the following morning. I also tell students that if they email me on a weekend, they can expect a response on Monday morning. This led to a better work/life balance and I no longer feel as overwhelmed with emails.

Never Yell (Ever)

The last piece of advice about communicating efficiently is never to yell at your students. Again, there is not a specific study that supports my opinion on this matter. My ideas about "yelling" at students are from observing other teachers in the classroom and hallways. Yelling at students does not benefit you or them. I have seen too many teachers get caught up in always "yelling" at students as their main way of disciplining them. When teachers use yelling as their main tool of discipline, students will ultimately only respond to that instructor when they yell, which creates a less than ideal situation. When you need to get the attention of your class or a specific student, use an alternative to yelling. I have never yelled or raised my voice to discipline a student, and I have strong classroom management. Of course, there will be frustrating moments in your teaching career, but please remember to not yell. It will make you a less effective communicator with your students and it will take too much energy out of you.

Final Thoughts

Being an effective communicator with coworkers, students, parents, and supervisors makes your first year of teaching easier. Having an "email plan" simplifies the methods by which people communicate with you and how you communicate with them. You will not have to waste time each day checking more than one work email address. Creating email contact lists to communicate with parents and guardians of students allows for you to open channels of communication with struggling students. Instead of spending an enormous amount of time typing in the emails of parents, you will be able to use your contact list to send out materials and course updates within minutes. By the time "Back to School Night" occurs, many parents and guardians will have received numerous emails from you. Your winning system will be on full display to all attendees of Back to School Night because you will have a clear plan on how to conduct the event in your classroom and how to introduce yourself. Communicating effectively with students contributes to the success of a classroom. Yelling at students leads to ineffective communication, both in the present moment and in the future. Using alternative methods to garner attention will allow for you to have the "keys" to communicate in a meaningful and effective way. Using specific phrasing during parent–teacher conferences will allow for you to have productive conversations with parents and guardians on how to help their student succeed in your classroom. Communicating effectively with students, parents, coworkers, and supervisors will contribute to you to winning your first year of teaching!

5

Contacting Parents/Guardians of Students

Establishing contact with the parents/guardians of students is extremely important as a teacher. When a student is misbehaving, not turning in work, or causing disruptions in your class, it is important to contact home to make them aware of their child's behaviors. When a student is doing extremely well in your class, it is important to contact home too. However, I will get to that in a bit. I always recommend that teachers email parents/guardians instead of calling when first establishing contact. Emails take less time to send and are more time-efficient. If you decide to call a parent, they may be on the phone with you for thirty minutes, which takes away your planning time. Another reason why emailing can serve better than calling home is that it is a lot easier to document the communication between the parent and yourself.

When to Just Pick Up the Phone

Sometimes, phone calls are better because a parent may be much ruder to you via email than when talking on the phone. If a parent is rude to you via email, I would suggest calling them to discuss what you need to communicate about their student. I would recommend having a supervisor present while you call the parent. It is always good to have someone there to vouch for you after the conversation. If you decide to include a supervisor on a phone call, inform the parent in an email that your supervisor will be on the call as well. This will ideally lead to clearer communication and for the parent to not feel taken off guard when they get on the call. You may also need to call home instead of emailing if a specific situation would be too difficult to explain over email. If you end up getting a rude email from a parent, my advice would be to respond "Thank you for your email" and leave it at that. If a parent does not ask a specific question, there is no reason to respond. Never get into an "email war" with a parent. An "email war" is when a parent and teacher have a contentious conversation over email that furthers their disagreements. If you feel like you are getting into an email war you have to accept that the prospects of a productive conversation are slim. If a parent asks to meet with you in person, I would recommend contacting your department chair, team leader, or administrator to be present at the meeting as an observer. I recommend never meeting with parents alone, especially if you feel like it is going to be a contentious meeting.

Staying Concise and Following Up

When emailing home about a student's misbehavior, make sure that your email is concise. The parent/guardian may not be receptive to you in the first place, so try to be brief. Regardless of the student's behavior in your class over the following few days, always send a follow-up email. In most cases the student's behavior will improve, and validating the improved behavior will likely increase their future good behavior in your class. When a student hears from their parent/guardian that their teacher emailed home stating that their behavior has improved, they will appreciate it and you will build more credibility with the student. Too often, teachers only email home when things are going wrong. It is important to take the time and make the effort to contact home when things are going well too.

Don't Forget the Praise

This brings me to my next point: there will be some students who, throughout their entire schooling, will never have a teacher reach out to tell their parents/guardians that they are doing well in school. As a first-year teacher, it may be hard to find the time to send emails praising students that are doing well in your class. However, contacting the parents of high-achieving students builds your credibility with their families and also shows the student that their hard work is appreciated in your classroom. Contacting parents and guardians of students should never be limited to informing them of negative issues. Sending a quick email highlighting the work of high-achieving students will reinforce their hard work in your class.

Alerting Parents to Bad Grades

Students who are struggling in your class may not be informing their parents of their grades. As a first-year teacher, I made the mistake of not informing parents of their child's D or E grade in my class the first marking period I ever taught. I received emails asking me about their child's grade and why they had not been contacted. This made me evaluate why, when, and how I was contacting the parents of students. If a student has a D or E after the first two weeks of the marking period, you should contact home. The email should include your name, class subject, grade, assignments the student is missing, and/or the assignments that led to the student receiving their current grade. By following the winning system, all of your assignments will be available digitally, so attaching them to an email will be easy. Emailing this information establishes the contact in writing and also allows for the parent/guardian to work with you to boost their child's grade in your class. You can also attach assignments for the child to work on. This saves you time spent giving them the assignment again in class if the parents can easily print the assignment at home. No matter what subject you teach, there is a good chance that a few students will receive a D or E grade in your subject regardless of your efforts. However, if you establish contact with home and work with those students to the best of your ability, you did your due diligence. Students may receive a D or E for a variety of personal, social, or academic reasons. But, as the teacher, it is your responsibility to do everything in your power to help raise their grades with their parents/guardians.

Final Thoughts

Establishing contact with the parents and guardians of your students can be difficult to navigate as a first-year teacher. However, contacting home through emails or phone calls is extremely important to do throughout the year. Knowing when to pick up the phone so as not to get into an "email war" with a parent will save you time and difficulty. Many parents/guardians have negative attitudes toward educators that were developed before their student was even in your class. If you start receiving difficult emails or phone calls from parents or guardians of students, you now have actionable steps to use when these situations arise. Again, do your best to keep most communication with parents/guardians through email. Having all communication in writing makes it extremely easy to document and keep track of any communication. However, if your email correspondence with a parent/guardian seems to be drifting into the "email war" territory, you now know when to pick up the phone. Including a supervisor on a phone call with a parent or guardian can potentially help you when dealing with difficult situations. Also, do not forget to alert parent/guardians of their student's grade if you think that the student may be at risk of not passing your class. Ideally, not all communication with parents/guardians will be about difficult situations. Sending two to three emails per week praising students to their parents/guardians will enhance your credibility in the school community. The emails serve an additional purpose of providing positive reinforcement to students in your class to continue their great work. Knowing how and when to contact the parents and guardians of your students will allow you to further develop your winning system.

6

Graduate School/Professional Development/Salary Advice

Being aware of the professional development opportunities that are available to you as a teacher is extremely important. Most school districts will pay you a higher salary once you obtain fifteen graduate credits, your master's degree, master's degree plus fifteen graduate credits, master's degree plus thirty graduate credits, master's degree plus forty-five graduate credits, master's degree plus sixty graduate credits, and your doctorate degree. When you are on the first rung of the salary scale, the starting salary between the different pay scales is not that significant. However, after ten years of teaching, the different salary scales make a huge difference to a teacher's income. In the example school district in Figure 6.1, if you have your master's degree you will earn roughly 14 percent more than a teacher without a master's degree after teaching ten years. If you are a teacher in the example district with a master's degree plus thirty graduate credits, you will earn roughly 18 percent more than a teacher with only a bachelor's degree. If you are a teacher in the example district with a master's degree plus sixty graduate credits, you will earn roughly 21 percent more than a teacher with only a bachelor's degree after teaching for ten years. As you can see, the financial difference between a teacher with a bachelor's degree compared to a teacher with a master's degree plus sixty credits is staggering. Figure 6.1 depicts a chart that I made to give a visual representation of the difference in salary after ten years for all four salary levels that I listed for the example school district.

<u>Example of a Salary Scale</u>

Salary Step (Years of Experience)	Bachelor's Degree	Master's Degree	Master's Degree + 30 graduate credits	Master's Degree + 60 graduate credits
1	$47,000	$51,000	$52,000	$54,500
10	$57,000	$64,980	$67,260	$68,970

Figure 6.1 Example of a salary scale. (A chart that describes the pay difference between a teacher in their first and tenth years based on having a college degree, graduate degree, graduate degree plus thirty credits, and graduate degree plus sixty credits.)

Boosting Your Salary and Pension

At the end of the day, we do not go into teaching for the money; however, it is important that you are aware of ways to boost your salary while also learning new things through professional development. Not only is the pension amount higher for the teacher with greater professional development credits, but their yearly salary will be higher as well. Most school districts will take a certain percentage of your paycheck to put in a state pension fund; the more money you contribute while working, the more money you will be paid each month when you retire. Depending on where you live, you may be able to join a teacher's union. If you can join a teacher's union, my advice would be to do so. There are numerous benefits to joining a union. One of those benefits is that they would be able to explain to you how the salary scale and pension program works by simply calling them. If you live in a "right to work" state, teaching unions are sometimes not allowed. However, you could always call your district's human resources department to ask questions about the salary scale.

Check for Continuing Ed Programs

Make sure you are aware of programs in your school district for continuing education for their employees. Not every school district is large, and they may not offer professional development. If your school district is large enough that they offer professional development classes that count toward credits on the salary scale, take as many of them as possible. They are typically cheaper than other options and allow you to go directly through your employer. However, most school districts have programs for tuition reimbursement. The old saying "you have to invest in yourself" is true. When a school district offers tuition reimbursement, take advantage of that. Usually, the way tuition reimbursement works is that you submit a request to your school district to get credits reimbursed for a specific graduate school program. Once they approve the program, you personally have to front the money to take graduate school courses as part of a master's program. Most school districts require that you receive a "B" grade or higher for them to reimburse the cost of that class. Also, most school districts will reimburse you for nine credits per year. Most graduate programs are thirty credits and completed in two years. Essentially, most school districts will reimburse you for 60 percent of your graduate program, which is a fantastic deal, once you graduate. Once you obtain your master's degree, your salary will go up. Therefore, by investing in yourself, you are able to make the money back that you spent.

Other Tips for Finding Good Grad Programs

To discuss graduate school in more depth, I would suggest enrolling in a program that will help enhance your career. Regardless if you want a leadership position one day, it is important that you choose your graduate programs wisely. I would recommend school leadership because it helps train teachers to one day become administrators. Even if you have no desire to be an administrator, you can use the experience gained while obtaining the degree to become a team leader or department chair. I also recommend looking at the costs of attending a graduate school program in person versus online. I was extremely naive about graduate school after I graduated from college and had no idea how many graduate programs could be completed online. Most online options for graduate school are significantly cheaper than going in-person to graduate school. Every person learns differently, but I would recommend accessing an online graduate school to save money and time. Again, every person is different. I recommend looking into both options.

Final Thoughts

Investing in yourself by taking professional development courses will allow you to build upon your winning system. Each year I try to take new professional development courses in a variety of subjects to broaden my horizons. During my first year of teaching I was enrolled in a graduate program and was able to interact with other first-year teachers. My discussions and experiences with my classmates provided me with different perspectives and ideas.

I do not advocate for every first-year teacher to enroll in a graduate school program; however, I do encourage first-year teachers to enroll in some form of professional development in their first year. In doing so, you will be exposed to different topics and roles in education. Your experiences in professional development will allow for you to have a clearer idea of what graduate programs you may enroll in or what other roles may interest you in the future. Again, we do not enter the field of education for a high salary. However, it is important for every first year teacher to be aware of the different salary scales that their district has so that you can invest in yourself. Many districts will pay for some or all of your schooling if you get high enough grades. Even if you have to front some of the costs, you will eventually make the money back when your salary increases. Choosing a professional development course or graduate program may seem overwhelming. Think about your winning system and what aspects of your system that you want to improve upon. This can lead you to the perfect professional development course for your needs. Investing in yourself will pay dividends and you will be able to enhance your winning system.

7

Expect to be Observed Frequently
How to Handle Formal and Informal Observations

Being observed in your first year of teaching can be nerve-racking, but expect it to happen – and happen frequently! You were hired because your school saw potential in you and believes that you can deliver high-quality instruction. However, since you are a first-year teacher, you will be monitored more closely than a veteran teacher. Observations should serve as a tool of growth for you in your teaching. Observations should not be used as a tool to make you feel like a bad teacher! You will be "informally" observed and "formally" observed throughout the entirety of your teaching career. Supervisors come into classrooms to collect data on calling practices, classroom management, teaching styles, student achievement, and much more. At the end of the day, your supervisors want to see that you can stand in front of a class and deliver effective instruction to students.

Informal Observations

Informal observations are not evaluative and happen frequently in schools across the county. An evaluative observation goes on your record, and typically will have a rubric or checklist that a supervisor uses to evaluate your teaching and student learning. Informal observations do not go on your "official" record and typically last between ten to fifteen minutes. Typically, your supervisor will sit in the back of the class and take notes on what you are doing. They might even walk around to hear students' discussions and peek at the assignment they are working on. When your supervisor walks in, do not panic! My first piece of advice is to continue teaching and do not stop your lesson. Stopping to address your supervisor breaks the flow of your lesson and makes it seem like you are not prepared to deliver instruction. Once your supervisor walks in, continue teaching your lesson, but hand them any materials/papers that students are working on for the day. This allows your supervisor to have the same materials as the students and gives them a better idea of what lesson you are teaching for the day. After giving your supervisor the papers from the lesson, continue teaching as nothing has changed. Do not do anything that you would not typically do, or attempt anything extravagant just to impress your supervisor. I have observed teachers in a lesson doing this, and students have wondered out loud "Why are they doing this? They never do that when Mr. Katzel isn't here!" Students will be brutally honest with adults at all times. If you start acting differently or teaching differently, it will be obvious to your supervisor and to your students. Most informal observations do not have follow-up discussions. Some supervisors may want to meet with you after an informal observation, but this is not too common. Most supervisors will leave a note in your mailbox or email you notes about your lesson. Typically, the feedback is short and has follow-up questions since they most likely will not see the entirety of the lesson. Always answer follow-up questions, and make sure to respond to your supervisor within one business day. This fosters a good working relationship with your supervisor, and they will appreciate your promptness in responding to their questions.

Formal Observations

Formal observations go on your record and should be taken seriously. Most school districts "formally" observe first-year teachers four to five times per year to ensure that they are capable of teaching students. Do not view formal observations as a "gotcha." No supervisor or school district conducts formal observations to try to fire teachers. Formal observations are in place to ensure that our students are receiving high-quality instruction from effective teachers. Most formal observations occur for the entirety of the class period so that the supervisor can see what a full lesson looks like in your room. The following tips I am about to give should be performed each class period regardless of whether your lesson is being observed or not. These steps should be part of your "winning system."

1   The first thing you should do is hand any papers or materials that your students are using for the day to your supervisor.

2   Second, start the class by verbalizing the objective for the day to the class so they know exactly what they will be learning. Part of your winning system (mentioned in Chapter 1) requires you to have your objective on the board when students walk in. However, reading the learning objective to the class is good practice and your supervisor will be looking for your objective as well.

3   The next step is to go over the warm-up with students and answer any questions they have about it.

4   After your warm-up, dive right into the lesson. Do not only call on students who have their hand up; also call on students who do not have their hand up. Your supervisor will be looking at your calling practices. It is important to not call on the same two students thirty times in one period!

5   Next, make sure you are circulating the classroom at all times or have a table set up where students can come up and ask for help. I usually circulate the classroom for the entirety of the class period. I sit down when I am going over things on the board or if I pull a chair up to a student's desk if they ask me a question. No supervisor wants to see a teacher sit in their chair the entire class period, so try to circulate throughout the classroom when you can. Whether you are being formally observed or teaching a regular lesson, make sure you provide time for students to talk to each other and that you have a clear "I do," "we do," and "you do." I include an "I do," "we do," "you do" in there because your supervisor wants to see you teach! When you are being observed it is not okay to just give a worksheet without giving directions and hope for the best. Regardless of whether you are being observed or not, you should always clearly model the activity, skill, or concept you are going over. Then make time to answer any questions before asking students in the class to help you with the next question or problem. I would advise calling students up to the board to encourage further participation. After you complete the "we do," have students complete the "I do."

Use (and Save!) Clear Data

Make sure you do not throw away any papers from the observed lesson and have graded work from the lesson that you were "formally" observed in. Having clear data is important for your supervisor to see and for you to analyze. Most supervisors will have a "post-observation conference" where they go over the observation with you and ask about the lesson. Having clear data to prove student achievement is important and shows the effectiveness of your teaching. Having data allows you to clearly lay out the next steps you will take in your lessons and how you will catch students up who did not meet the objective for the lesson you taught. Your supervisor will want to hear you talk about all of this in your post-observation conference, but it is always best practice if you do this after each lesson, regardless if you are being observed or not. Your supervisor will be impressed if you discuss data in your post-observation conference. For example, if you analyzed the exit cards from your class, you can easily calculate who "met the objective" and who "did not meet the objective." If you have twenty-five students in a class and twenty "met the objective," you then know you have five students who "did not meet the objective," and you can provide your supervisor with graded work and data in the post-conference. You can state "80 percent of my students met the objective, while 20 percent did not meet the objective. I will ensure that 20 percent of the students are retaught the skill/concept in the next class by conducting a small group where I can work more closely with them." Having clear data and a plan to catch up students who are behind helps your supervisor see that you were reflective in the lesson that you were supervised in. Again, you should always do this regardless of whether you are being observed. However, it is important to verbalize these thoughts and ideas to your supervisor, so they see that you are data-driven and care about student achievement in your classes.

Don't Take Criticism Personally

My last piece of advice for informal and formal observations is to not take criticism personally. Some supervisors are very tactful in how they give feedback, while others are not. Feedback from supervisors may seem like criticism or a personal attack. At the end of the day, your supervisor wants you to grow as a teacher and for your students to achieve success in your classroom. You must give your supervisor the benefit of the doubt when they give you feedback. Even if they are not tactful in how they give the feedback, try to reflect on how their feedback can make you a better teacher. Regardless of how you are delivered feedback, thank your supervisor and try to implement ideas that they have for your classroom. Sending an email about how you implemented their feedback would go a long way. It shows that you are receptive to feedback and willing to try new things.

Final Thoughts

Being informally and formally observed can be a nerve-racking experience during your first year of teaching. If you have a difficult supervisor, classroom observations may not be pleasant. However, you are now equipped with actionable steps to enhance your observations. As soon as a supervisor or observer walks into the room, you now know to immediately hand them classroom materials. Informal observations will occur numerous times throughout your first year. I was informally observed at least once a week for the entirety of my first year of teaching. Formal observations typically occur between three and five times per year. By having a winning system in place, it will not matter what class period or lesson is observed by a supervisor. Regardless of whether you are being observed or not, collecting data on the effectiveness of your lesson allows for you to further meet the needs of your students and also your supervisor. Whether it be through an email or in a meeting, you now know to present clear data from the lesson that was observed. Meetings with supervisors are less intimidating when you have data and a clear plan on how you will utilize the collected data to enhance student achievement. Some supervisors may give feedback in a way that is not tactful. However, take their feedback seriously and analyze how their feedback can be used to improve your teaching.

8

Dealing with Difficult Coworkers or Supervisors

Regardless of what industry you are in or where you work, you are going to have difficult coworkers and/or supervisors. The best advice I can give to new teachers is to not "take the bait." As a new person in the building, your coworkers are going to try to feel you out and see who you are. Some of your coworkers may try to ask personal questions, even if they do not know you well. If you do not wish to talk about your personal life, do not answer their questions and say you don't feel comfortable talking about that. Whether it be relationships, family, or something as simple as how your weekend was, if you do not feel like talking about it, don't. Some people have pure intentions and want to get to know you, but others don't. Be careful how much you tell people about your personal life. Your political and religious beliefs are not anyone else's business. Too often, I see coworkers bring up these topics with each other. As someone that is new in the building, scope out the staff and get a feel for the people around you. Obviously, if you feel that you can trust a coworker, by all means be open about your life. However, make sure you feel comfortable with what you are saying potentially getting back to you. For example, one time I told a coworker I was going to Canada for a week during winter break. When I got back from the trip, more than five people who I barely knew asked me about the trip. It was quite odd, and I wasn't a fan of everyone knowing my business.

Mixing Colleagues and Social Media

This leads me to my next topic: social media. Only add coworkers on social media that you feel comfortable seeing everything about your life on social media. If someone requests you on social media and you do not want them to see your page, leave their "request" unanswered. If they bring it up, say you do not check social media often. You have every right to keep your private life private.

Avoiding Draining or Hostile Emails

Receiving emails from coworkers or supervisors is a normal part of the job. Sometimes you may receive an off-putting email. If no direct question is asked, simply respond with "Thank you for your email." It is hard to do this in the heat of the moment, but it is not worth getting into an "email war" with anyone and taking their bait. If you get into an "email war" with a coworker you won't win in the long run, even if you win that particular disagreement. Going back and forth through email is draining and distracts you throughout the day. The best move you can make is to not engage with coworkers over email, especially if they are hostile toward you.

Don't Let it Affect Your Work

As a first-year teacher, there are many different factors that impact your day. Learning a new curriculum, making copies, grading papers, planning, and so much more go into just one day of teaching during your first year. At the end of the day, we are all human beings and rude comments or bad interactions with coworkers or supervisors will affect how you feel. However, we must persevere and learn to shrug off negative comments. Some teachers become jaded toward students, coworkers, and education in general. For example, I once had a colleague who would constantly comment on my clothing and tell me I was "too dressed up" because I wore a tie. The purpose of commenting on my clothes and desire to wear a tie to work was to make me feel uncomfortable and change my behavior. If you feel like wearing nice clothes to work, wear nice clothes. Each time a comment was made on my choice of clothing, I said "Thanks for noticing my clothes." I left it at that because I did not want to let somebody else's negativity impact my choices and how I went about my day. This mindset was developed over time through practice.

During my first year of teaching, I had a supervisor make a negative comment about a recent haircut. I spent the next planning period unfocussed and upset, only thinking about the comment that they had made to me. Instead of grading thirty papers, I sat at my desk and stewed over the comments. I was able to shake the comment off by the time students returned to class, but I wasted a lot of time that day over a simple comment! Whatever is said by someone that you work with, don't let it affect your work.

Final Thoughts

Dealing with difficult supervisors and coworkers is an unfortunate part of working in any field or profession. Adding coworkers or supervisors on social media potentially allows people to get an intimate look at your life. I highly recommend not adding anyone from work to your social media until you are 100 percent comfortable with them and trust their intentions. To further expand on social media, I recommend keeping all of your pages set to "private." Having your social pages open to the public means that students, colleagues, and parents can view whatever you post. Also, email wars are not limited to parents and guardians – teachers easily can get into "email wars" amongst themselves as well! Remember to not take the bait with any coworkers that send nasty emails. In an ideal situation, you will be part of a school that is welcoming and kind toward first-year teachers. However, developing a winning system throughout the course of your first year will lessen the impact that difficult coworkers and supervisors have on your daily experiences.

9

Teaching Sixth Grade
Helping with Social Changes

Being a sixth-grade teacher is an extremely rewarding position to be in as a first-year educator! Most school districts are structured so that sixth grade is the first year in middle school. Handling change can be difficult for any person regardless of their age or profession, especially when change is drastic. As an educator who has worked with thousands of sixth-grade students and parents, I can tell you the hardest thing for a sixth-grade student to adapt to is all of the change that middle school brings. Most sixth-grade students go from having one or two fifth-grade teachers to having six to seven teachers. In some cases, there are between two to five feeder elementary schools per middle school, which means that a sixth-grade student will be have an entirely new set of peers compared to elementary school. An average elementary school in a mid-sized school district has about 150 students in each grade level. An average middle school in a mid-sized district has about 350 students in each grade level. Having all of the sixth-grade students that have not met before meet each other leads to unanticipated consequences. Social circles grow or shrink, friendships don't last, friendships evolve, and students sometimes do not adapt well to the change. Now, you must be thinking, "Why is he mentioning this?" The reason is all of the things I just listed happen in the first week of middle school for sixth-grade students! Social factors impact what happens in your classroom, for better or for worse. Keeping in mind that sixth grade involves social change along with academic changes will allow you to better develop and manage expectations inside and outside of the classroom for sixth-grade students.

Using Parent Communications Effectively

Before the first week of classes, I recommend sending an email to all of the parent/guardians of your sixth-grade students. Figure 9.1 provides an example.

Email Title: Welcome Back to XXXXXX Middle School and to Mr. Katzel's Class!

Dear Parent(s)/Guardian(s),

As your child's history teacher this year, I would like to introduce myself. My name is Mr. Katzel and I have taught at XXXX Middle School for the past four years. In addition to teaching, I serve as one of the Team Leaders.

I have a strong belief that a partnership between teachers and parent/guardians leads to students achieving their highest potential. By working together, we are going to make this a rememberable year! I invite you to email me anytime that you have a question regarding your child's progress in school.

I will be assigning assignments through the "XXXX Classroom Portal". When I assign work, I will use the acronyms of "DD" and "DL". The "DD" stands for the assignment's due date. While the "DL" stands for the deadline for the assignment to be turned in. The deadline is the last day that an assignment can be completed for credit.

Please let me know if you have any questions. I am looking forward to a great year!

Thank You,

Mr. Katzel

Figure 9.1 Welcome back to school message. (An example email that a sixth-grade teacher can send to parents and guardians during the first week of school that introduces who the teacher is and what subject they teach.)

Having consistent communication with the parents of your sixth-grade students is extremely important. I recommend sending reminders about homework, classwork, and projects to all sixth grade parents/guardians. Many schools have online systems that make it easy to send messages to all parents/guardians of the students that you teach. I try to limit the amount I write in each update to further enhance the point or message I want to get across. The saying "less is more" rings very true when sending communications to sixth grade parents. Parents of sixth-grade parents are used to dealing with one to three teachers per year in elementary school, and are now dealing with seven middle school teachers! It can be overwhelming reading emails from each teacher, multiple times per week. That is why I recommend being concise in your communication and sending only one "mass" classroom update per week.

A Big Year of Growth

Making the transition from fifth grade to sixth grade allows a lot of room for students to grow. What is special about sixth grade is that you can see a significant amount of growth in one short year, for a variety of factors. Sixth-grade students are "new middle school students." I always advise sixth-grade teachers to start the year with the mindset of having a "blank slate." Some incoming sixth graders had bad experiences in elementary school and think that teachers "know about me," "know I can't do xyz," or "know that I am bad." These ideas were not magically put in the student's head: the actions or words of an adult influenced the student to think of themselves in a certain way, or that they are "bad." I highly recommend mentioning the idea of a "blank slate" the entirety of the first month you teach sixth graders. This reassures the students that they have a fresh start with you and that their past is important but does not define who they are as a student in your classroom. The point I am making is that students in sixth grade can "flip the script" on how they feel about school, or at minimum how they feel about school while they are in your class, based solely on how you interact with them and respond to comments about "what happened in fifth grade."

Creating a Sense of Community

I wanted to delve into the mindsets of sixth-grade students to provide insight into what occurs at the start of middle school. Again, you will be one of six or seven teachers for each student. Establishing a sense of community is extremely important when teaching sixth grade. Students are in a new school, with new peers, new teachers, and new routines. Having to wake up earlier in the morning can throw off the student's schedule. As stated earlier in the book, establishing a winning system is extremely important during the first week of school. However, I want to speak to the specifics of sixth grade and what to do the first week of school to establish a classroom community to better integrate students to your classroom and middle school. Conducting "icebreakers" throughout the first week of school allows students in your class to become more familiar with their peers. When adults are asked to do icebreakers during a meeting, they definitely are not thrilled! Keeping this in mind, I suggest not referring to such activities as "icebreakers" to your class. Frame the activity so that it has a clear purpose to the students. For example, "We are now going to conduct classmate interviews to further develop our classroom community." I also suggest allocating a specific amount of time

Name_____   **Date**_____   **Period**_____

Interview Form

Name of person who is being interviewed:

1. What is one goal that you have for the 20XX-20XX school year?

2. What was your favorite part of summer vacation?

3. In your opinion, what is the best way to achieve a goal in school?

Name of person who is being interviewed:

1. What is one goal that you have for the 20XX-20XX school year?

2. What was your favorite part of summer vacation?

3. In your opinion, what is the best way to achieve a goal in school?

Name of person who is being interviewed:

1. What is one goal that you have for the 20XX-20XX school year?

2. What was your favorite part of summer vacation?

3. In your opinion, what is the best way to achieve a goal in school?

Figure 9.2 Student interview assignment. (An assignment for students to interview their peers about a goal they have, how their summer break went, and how to achieve a specific goal.)

each class period during the first week of school to "icebreaker" activities. For example, each school year I allocate a chunk of time on the second day of school for sixth-grade students to interview three of their classmates. Figure 9.2 provides an example of an interview worksheet I give to students during the first week of school.

I purposely have students interview three classmates so that they branch out and meet their peers. I allot five minutes per student interview and cap the assignment at three interviews. I make it very clear that students cannot interview the same classmate more than once. It is easy for students to interview someone they already know or a friend in their class. However, by providing three interview slots, I am hoping they interact with at least one person that they do not know. An activity such as "student interviews" builds the capacity of a classroom community to grow since students are interacting with each other in a social and an academic way. Every teacher has students that are quiet and do not like to talk. This activity allows for the "quieter" students to build their social and verbal skills by interacting with other students. I always allow students to choose their own partners for this activity for each five minute interview.

This "icebreaker" activity also allows you to make observations about your new students based on how students interact with each other. This activity highlights which students have a large social circle: "Student John Doe had six classmates approach him to conduct the interview, which shows he has a large social circle." This activity also allows you to see which students are leaders: "Student Jane Doe volunteered to partner up with the Student Kim Doe, who had no partner to work with for the interview." And this activity reveals which students struggle with following directions: "Bill Doe tried interviewing Matt Doe again after I asked him not to." This activity also shows which students may struggle socially with their peers: "During all three rounds of interviews, I noticed that Student B struggled finding a partner each round."

This icebreaker helps sixth-grade teachers develop a winning system for their classroom. To be clear, how students act during one icebreaker does not define who they are or how they will act for the entirety of the year. However, it does allow you to make inferences and educated assessments of the personalities that you will have in your specific class period. This icebreaker activity should leave you with a general idea of the social capacity and make-up of your class period. This icebreaker activity also assists you to help students in their transition to middle school. If you noticed one or more students struggling to interact and find partners during the icebreaker, you can write their names down to recommend them for a lunch group or "lunch bunch." Most middle schools have "lunch bunches" that are organized by the counseling department. School guidance counselors often get student groups together during lunch to promote social skills and relationship building amongst sixth-grade students. I have seen so many students make friends through "lunch bunches." In middle school, finding one friend can make a world of difference for students. Over the years, it is powerful looking back at how many students benefited from structured social gatherings at school based upon my own and my fellow teachers' recommendations to the group. I want to mention that it is very possible that those students have social connections outside of the students in that specific class period; however, it does not hurt recommending them to a group to boost their social skills.

Helping with the Development of Social Skills

Kindergarten, sixth grade, and twelfth grade are transitional years for students. There is so much that can be covered in this chapter about sixth-grade students due to the transitional nature of this year. However, as previously stated, the intention of this book is not to overpower you with information – my intention is to empower you with tools that are applicable, easy to use, and have purpose. I plan on covering more tips and ideas that can be implemented in your sixth grade classroom that you can use without the feeling of being overwhelmed. Throughout sixth grade, I believe that is important to focus on developing the social skills of your students. Incorporating discussions in your classroom lesson plans differentiates your instruction, allows for the lesson to be student centered, and develops the social skills of students. I recommend having a structured student discussion at least once each marking period to enable students to develop their public speaking and social skills. Too many sixth-grade students were allowed to not actively participate in elementary school because their teachers gave them a "pass" since they always completed their work. In the real world, regardless of your job, you have to talk with other people and have discussions. You may be thinking right now "My subject does not allow for a class discussion because of the content." I hope that after you read this chapter and look at the resources below, you change your mind. You can design a class discussion based around any subject. If you are a physical education teacher, you can give out an article relevant to your subject, have students read the article, and then come up with discussion questions. If you teach math, you can hand out an article about a specific mathematician and develop discussion questions as well. The point of the discussion is not particularly the topic, or the article/reading students need to complete: it is the discussion itself. Setting the stage for the discussion is extremely important.

- **The set-up**: First, set your room up so that there is a circle of desks that are the "inner circle" and a circle of desks surrounding the inner circle that is called the "outer circle." Telling students that each of their voices is valued is the first step.
- **Ground rules:** Next, discuss the difference between an argument and a discussion. A class discussion should not devolve into an argument, and you will serve as the moderator to ensure that this does not happen. Developing ground rules that work for the discussion is extremely important. I would have the rules up on the board while the discussion takes place.
- **Groups and partners:** Now, you may be thinking, "I have 30 students in my class, how will I have a discussion with thirty students at once?" To solve this problem, there will be a total of two classroom discussions. There will be "group one" and "group two," so that the class is split in half. The teacher pre-assigns which group a student is in and the student's partner. Another component of the discussion is that each student is partnered up. Each student will give their "partner"

feedback at the end of class. An example worksheet for this is given in Figure 9.4. The purpose of partnering-up students is to allow for student-to-student feedback to occur. The "Student Partner Sheet" won't be used for a grade. Rather, it is used for students to engage with one another.

◆ **Time allotments:** To allow sufficient time for the discussion, allocate 15 minutes for each group. Awkward silences are okay! Make sure students know that regardless of how much they talk, they will have 15 minutes to discuss each question and ask each other questions that they developed. Make it clear that when a student's group is having their discussion, they are the "inner circle," and when students are not in the discussion, they are observing their partner in the "outer circle."

◆ **Student feedback:** At the end of class, provide 5 minutes for each "partner group" to give feedback. Student-to-student feedback can be hard to create; this lesson gives plenty of chances for this, and it promotes student collaboration (Figures 9.3 and 9.4).

5. Themes of Geography Discussion

Name: Group 1 or 2 (Circle)

Question	Answer (3-4 sentences)	Question(s) for the Class
1. How does geography impact your life?		
2. Which theme of geography is the most important? Please explain.		
3. Which theme of geography is the least important? Please explain.		

Figure 9.3 Five themes of geography classroom discussion assignment. (An assignment that asks discussion questions to prompt students to engage in academic discourse.)

Discussion Observation Checklist

Your Name: Partner's Name:

Put a tally mark each time your partner..	Notes about the Discussion
Speaks in the discussion:	
Refers to the reading/article:	
Asks a question to a classmate:	
Responds to another speaker:	

Figure 9.4 Discussion Observation Checklist. (A paper that allows for students to keep track how many times their discussion partner spoke in the discussion, referred to an article, asked a question, or responded to another speaker.)

Final Thoughts

When teaching sixth-grade students, it is always important to try to incorporate social aspects into your lessons. In my personal opinion, social skills should be the theme of the year. Sixth grade is a year of transition for students and parents alike. Having a winning system in place will help you succeed throughout the school year. It is easy to forget that some sixth-grade students do not turn eleven until well into the school year. Never lower your expectations, and stay consistent with your winning system. Sixth-grade students do not have any preconceived notions of middle school and what a specific teacher or subject should be like. Treat each day with the "blank slate" mentality and your success in teaching sixth grade will only be enhanced. This book is only a launching pad for you to develop and create ideas for your classroom. Sixth-grade students crave interactions with their peers, and providing academic opportunities for them to interact with their peers will strengthen their effort and performance in your classroom. Your winning system will provide them with the proper introduction to secondary school and what can be expected of them as a new student in middle school.

10

Teaching Seventh Grade
Conscious Repetition

I would argue that being a seventh-grade teacher puts you in a position to make unique impact that neither sixth- or eighth-grade teachers can have on a middle school student. I am not advocating that sixth- or eighth-grade teachers cannot have the same impact on their students as a seventh-grade teacher. Rather, I am stating that a seventh-grade teacher is in a unique position because they are teaching students who have had one year of experience in middle school and who still have a year left of middle school. This allows seventh-grade teachers to develop a unique mindset on how they teach and work with students throughout the school year. I always refer to the term "conscious repetition" when I teach seventh-grade students and work with seventh-grade teachers and parents of seventh-grade students. If you were to look up conscious repetition in a search engine, you would find a definition that has to do with repeating something over and over again until whatever is being repeated is remembered. That definition of conscious repetition is not what I have in mind when working with seventh-grade students. What conscious repetition means for teachers is having the mindset that you are going to make the conscious decision to help students academically and socially by using different methods to meet the same goal repeatedly throughout the school year. Seventh-grade students crave structured routines but have difficulty with the repetition of how assignments are structured. Here are some examples.

Exit Tickets

In my years teaching seventh grade, I made sure to vary how I conducted formative assessments or "exit tickets." One exit ticket was to draw a short cartoon summarizing a historical topic of the day. Another exit ticket could be a series of multiple-choice questions or "fill in the blank" questions. The point I am trying to make is I was using my mindset of "conscious repetition" when designing lessons. Each day I was assessing student's knowledge of a topic, but consciously changing the structures of how students show me they that had understood the topic. Throughout my classroom observations of teachers in general, I noticed that some teachers can get caught up in using the same formative assessments. Seventh-grade students are known to quote the famous "Why do we have to do this again?." Through the use of conscious repetition, students are not completing the same type of assignments each time. However, students are repetitively demonstrating what they learned each class through the exit tickets. Formative assessments are one of many topics that encompass the conscious repetition mindset.

Student Autobiography

Another strategy that can be used through the lens of conscious repetition is an activity called "My Autobiography." The "My Autobiography" assignment can be implemented throughout the school year as a short "wellness check." Wellness checks are informal check-ins with seventh-grade students to see how they are doing socially and emotionally, and to see what areas of school they need help in. Of course, this can be done through teacher observation and when teachers greet students each day. However, some students may have a smile on their face each day but could very well be struggling mightily. Allowing students an alternative outlet to check in with you is extremely important. Verbalizing thoughts and emotions can be difficult even for adults, so providing an alternative outlet to check in with you in seventh grade is imperative. Many elementary and middle school teachers keep a jar or box on their desk where students can write a note to them. This is too frequently used as the only method for students to check in with a teacher in a somewhat discrete manner, minus meeting one-on-one or having a quiet conversation in class. Many students may be afraid that their peers will listen or hear what they want to express. Also, it may be embarrassing for a student to stand up and put a note in a box because they will not want their peers to see them do this. That is why the "My Autobiography" assignment is so important. Figures 10.1 and 10.2 provide examples of the "My Autobiography" assignment for the first week of school and for the end of the first semester, respectively. I will explain the rationale for the questions on the worksheets, and the reason why this assignment should be done at least twice during seventh grade, in the next paragraph.

The "My Autobiography" assignment has four questions. I always ask, "How would you describe yourself using one word?" for a specific purpose. Students may put an answer such as "sad," "happy," "excited," "tired," "energetic," or many other words. Typically, when seventh-grade students see this question, they describe how they feel in that particular moment. I like putting that question at the beginning of the assignment to "warm up" student thinking. Asking the question "How would you describe yourself as a student in 2–3 sentences?" allows students to further reflect on who they are and what they are about. If a student has low self-esteem or a negative attitude toward school, it will come out in their answer to this question. This allows the teacher to see what the student believes about themselves as a learner and use this information when interacting and teaching the student. For example, if a student answers, "I am not good at school and never have been. I am not a good student," a seventh-grade teacher knows that they should take steps to build up the confidence of that student throughout the year: perhaps something as simple as mentioning to the class that you "enjoyed reading Student A's autobiography and are looking forward to a great year." Obviously, you do not share what the student specifically said, but positive recognition is a good start in building the confidence of a student who views themselves as a "bad student" or "not good at school." Asking the question "What is a challenge that you have overcome in your life?" allows a student a chance to let their teacher know of any extenuating circumstances if they choose to do so. Not every student is going to spill their heart out on a worksheet. However, some students may tell you of any difficulties that are going on at home or school. This gives you the chance to learn more about a student and to be more aware of what is occurring in their lives. Providing a nonverbal opportunity for students to express any challenges in their lives is extremely important. For example, a student wrote about their mother living in a different country, which led to the student being responsible for watching their siblings after school. The student then wrote about how completing a huge art project in sixth grade was the challenge that they overcame, because they had to always babysit their siblings. With this knowledge, I understood the circumstances that my student faced each day. Each time there was a homework assignment or project, I ensured that this student had a paper copy and knew where it was located online. I was being conscious of their circumstances at home, while being "repetitive" in giving them another way to complete homework (either online or by paper). Asking the question, "What does success in seventh grade look like to you?" prompts students to tell you a bit more about themselves. Over the years, students have mentioned sporting accomplishments, social accomplishments, or academic accomplishments as their goals. Some students see success as doing well in sports. Other students view success as more academic, such as "making the honor roll" or "getting straight As." Other students may put "make a new friend since I am new to the school this year." Having an understanding of what success looks like to each student allows you to get to know them. If a student answers that they want to make friends, you could help them out by submitting their name to a club sponsor or guidance counselor to put them in a social "lunch bunch" group. The point of this assignment is to get to know students and provide information to the teacher to better inform them of who they teach. This initial assignment is also used as a "social-emotional check in" because it allows students to write about anything that is bothering them, if they choose to do so. It is extremely important to keep a copy of every "My Autobiography" assignment so that students can look at what they initially wrote while completing the "Mid-Year Autobiography." The "Mid-Year Autobiography" assignment allows a teacher to use the mindset of conscious repetition. I intentionally structured the "Mid-Year Autobiography" to be similar to the "My Autobiography" assignment in order to conduct a social/emotional check-in on students and to serve as a follow up to the "My Autobiography" assignment from the first week of school. By having a "mid-year check-in," teachers are also providing students a chance to reflect on how their year is going, who they were at the start of the year, and who they are now. Middle school students' feelings toward school can change rapidly. Providing them the chance to view what they wrote the first week of school before reflecting on themselves mid-year provides a powerful juncture for students to think about how their year is progressing. I tweaked all of the questions to include room for students to comment on their first semester. Students will again be able to notify teachers of any difficult circumstances that are occurring. After looking at the "Mid-Year Autobiography" I make sure to give both papers back to the student and write a short note thanking them for their answers. While the "My Autobiography" assignment is a very direct way to check in with students, there are other ways to check in with your seventh-grade students as well. This is just one tool you can use to get to know your students better and check in with them.

First Week of School-Autobiography

Name_____   Date_____

Question	How would you describe yourself using one word?	How would you describe yourself as a student in 2-3 sentences?	What is a challenge that you have overcome in your life?	What does success in seventh grade look like to you?
Answer				

Figure 10.1 Autobiography Assignment. (An assignment that a teacher can give students during the first week of school that asks them to describe themselves and what factors would lead to a successful year in seventh grade.)

End of First Semester-Autobiography

Name_____   Date_____

Question	How would you describe yourself using one word?	How would you describe yourself in 2-3 sentences? Is this similar or different than what you put at the start of the year?	What is a challenge that you have overcome in the first semester of school?	How have you changed as a student since the first day of seventh grade?
Answer				

Figure 10.2 End-of-Semester Autobiography. (An assignment that a teacher can give students during the last week of the first semester of school to follow up on the first "Autobiography" assignment administered during the first week of school.)

Final Thoughts

Teaching seventh grade is always fun! Do not assume that they remember everything from sixth grade. Start the school year with some basics and do not assume that all of your students have the same foundational knowledge. Some students in seventh grade could be coming from different school districts. Do not be afraid of taking academic risks with seventh-grade students. Using the conscious repetition mindset, you know that providing different avenues for success is important. Using the conscious repetition mindset, you know that changing up how you implement lessons is important as well. Seventh-grade students feel that they are no longer the "young kids" and want to be challenged academically (even if they do not admit it). You will have a lasting impact on your students' academic success in seventh grade and beyond by using a winning system that emphasizes consistency and structure.

11

Teaching Eighth Grade
Solution-Based Learning

Eighth grade students are in an interesting position since they have been in middle school for two years and are getting ready to enter high school the next year. Many students find themselves feeling apathetic toward school and being in class in general. This is the reason that teaching eighth grade excites me so much. I have the opportunity to reenergize student attitudes toward school, and my classroom specifically. Depending on a student's experience of sixth and seventh grade, they may have bad feelings toward a specific subject in school. Being an eighth-grade teacher provides a chance to change student perceptions about a subject by implementing a winning system in your classroom. Eighth-grade students can handle a bit more autonomy in their learning than their younger peers. In my experience if teaching eighth grade, I have noticed that eighth-grade students do not do well with monotonous assignments in class. What I mean by "monotonous assignments" is constantly assessing students a specific way, always starting class with certain activity, or having every homework assignment be a reading activity. Having "monotonous assignments" will lead to student disengagement and apathy. That is what we do not want in a classroom. I like to call eighth grade "the turning point" because this is the year where teachers can push eighth-grade students to turn a corner to academic success by embracing their desire for greater autonomy. Providing eighth-grade students with multiple avenues to express their learning will ideally allow eighth-grade students to be actively engaged in your classroom. There are dozens upon dozens of examples of how you can provide multiple avenues to eighth-grade students throughout the school year. Essentially, providing multiple avenues is allowing students to choose from two or more options to demonstrate their learning for a topic. I will give you a clear example of what "multiple avenues" look like so you can implement this practice with your eighth-grade class. Figure 11.1 provides an example from when I taught eighth-grade social studies.

Name: _____ Date: _____
Period: _____
Choice: _____

<u>Student Choice Exit Ticket</u>

Directions: You may choose ONE of the two options below to show your learning. You do NOT have to complete both assignments. Use the next page to complete one of the assignments below.

1. Social Media Page—Make a social media profile for a historical figure during the British colonization of the United States. Your profile must have at least 2 the following 5 vocabulary terms mentioned on the page: King, Monarchy, Stamp Act, Trade, Famine. You can choose the location/time of the profile.

2. Cartoon—Draw a cartoon summarizing a day in the life of an American colonist after spending their first month in one of the colonies.

Figure 11.1 Social Media Page or Cartoon Exit Ticket. (An assignment that asks students to either make a social media page for a historical figure during the British colonization of North America or draw a cartoon of the daily life of an American colonist.)

Collapse of the Soviet Union

Name: **Date:**   **Period:**

The year is 1991 and the Soviet Union just fell apart. 14 new countries just broke apart from the Soviet Union and you have to think fast. As the leader of the new <u>democratic</u> Russia you have a lot of decisions to make. The United States has reached out to you and offered their help. Now the question is do you trust them?

The first step you have is to figure out things about your own country before deciding what you are going to do.

1. What is your countries name?
   Russia or come up with a new name

2. 14 new countries broke apart from the Soviet Union. Should Russia try to get them to become part of the new Russia? Explain your reasoning.

3. What is the capital of non-communist Russia? (Come up with the name)

4. Now that communism is gone how soon will you decide to start elections to elect leaders? Should elections be right away? Should they be in a year so that the country has time to organize?

5. Should you accept help from communis China even though you are the leader of the new non-communist Russia?

6. What should the new democratic government do with the ole communist leaders? Should they be jailed or allowed to live freely? Explain your reasoning.

7. The United States has reached out and offered to help your country since you are no longer communist. Should the United States be an ally now that Russia is democratic and not communist? Explain your reasoning by citing reasons from what you have learned in class. (Answer in a paragraph of at least 7 sentences)

Figure 11.2 Collapse of the Soviet Union Assignment. (An assignment asking students to make decision for a newly formed country as a result of the collapse of the Soviet Union. Students are asked to make decisions on the structure of government and economy.)

Solution-Based Learning

I could write an entire book about the benefits of "student choice." However, for the purpose of this book, I want to give specific advice that can be implemented immediately in your classroom. An important aspect of teaching eighth grade is allowing students to engage in what I like to call "solution-based learning through group collaboration." I know that was very wordy! In eighth grade students are older and are at a point in their lives where peer interaction is crucial in keeping them focused in class. I highly recommend providing opportunities for eighth-grade students to work in groups with

Name_____

Budget Activity- Economic Depression

The month is February (a non-leap year) and there are 28 days you need to make a budget for! You have a tight budget for the month! You have $19.87 in your bank account and just got paid from work. Your paycheck just gave you $8.49 after taxes. This is where is gets tricky! This means that you have $28.36 to spend in the next month. You have to provide shelter, food, and water for your family. Your family consists of you, your brother, and two parents. Rent is due at the end of the month, and it costs $7 and must be paid on time. If you do not fill your car up with gas, you will have to walk 4 miles to work. Please items choose wisely!

1. Rent- $7
2. Milk- $2
3. Eggs (Enough for 1 week)- $.91
4. .5 Pound of Chicken Tenders- $.54
5. .5 Pound of Ground Beef- $.71
6. Electric Bill- $3.45
7. Cost of gas to fill up your car for a week- $1.24
8. Flour (For 2 pounds)- $2.34
9. Bag of Rice (10 Pounds)- $3.19
10. One Pound of Coffee (Enough for a month)- $3.42
11. Potatoes (2 Pounds)- $2.41
12. Bicycle- $5.68

***Please show all of your "math" work on the back of the paper.**

Figure 11.3 Budget Activity: Economic Depression. (An assignment asking students to develop a budget for their family during the Great Depression. Students have $19.87 to work with for the entire month of February.)

their peers to solve a problem that is relevant to your curriculum and subject matter. I also recommend pre-assigning groups of three to four students so that each student has a greater likelihood of giving their input. Groups larger than four are not ideal and can lead to students moving off task. Also, please change up the composition of the groups each time you do a group assignment. This allows for students to work with different partners and be exposed to different peers. A solution-based learning example in math class could be a teacher assigning a difficult math problem that is related to what is being taught. Before students can solve it on their own, the math teacher breaks the class up into groups and asks that each group makes a poster answering the problem and explaining their thought process. This allows students to bounce ideas off each other and work collaboratively. This also allows students to build social skills through solving a problem and having to discuss the matter with their classmates. This also gets eighth-grade students away of their desks and moving around the classroom, which breaks the monotony of the school day. Another aspect of the "solution-based learning" idea is to have each group present their poster. Allocating time for each group to present allows students to engage with their peers on a larger level and provides a chance for students to verbalize their thinking. Figures 11.2 and 11.3 provide examples of two "solution-based" learning activities I have done while teaching eighth-grade social studies where students then presented their work.

Final Thoughts

The point of this chapter was to give you inspiration to implement your own solution-based learning. Teaching eighth grade provides the unique challenge of inspiring students to grow academically while getting them ready for high school. By implementing a winning system as discussed earlier in the book, you will have a pathway to success. By giving your eighth-grade students more opportunities to work collaboratively and complete "solution-based assignments," you are encouraging them to make further connections with their peers while learning. Solution-based learning allows for your eighth-grade students to hear new ideas and different methods of thinking as a direct result of working in groups. Allowing eighth-grade students to complete assignments through different avenues will further engage them, and will allow them to feel that they have some control over their learning since they can choose how they respond to an assignment. Eighth grade is an amazing year that provides so many opportunities to enable students to grow both academically and as people. As their teacher, you will serve a large part your students' year. By having a winning system and implementing solution-based learning, you are getting them ready for high school and beyond.

12

Adapting to the Ever-Changing World
Tips for Virtual Learning during Pandemics and Beyond

Being a teacher requires the mindset of adaptability. Differentiating instruction, using behavior management techniques, answering questions, conducting small groups for re-teaches, and so many more things require teachers to adapt on a daily basis. School being forced to shift to online learning, such as during the 2020 Coronavirus pandemic, has further highlighted the importance of having a winning system. In Chapter 2, I discuss the benefits of short-term and long-term planning. If your school needs to move to online teaching, maintaining your system of short-term and long-term planning is even more important. Having all of your resources available digitally, through the cloud or on your computer, allows for you to more easily shift your classroom online. Looking up specific lesson plans based on the unit and day allows you to be more organized than a teacher who does not have most (or any) of their lesson plans saved online.

Allow Technology to Work for You

Using technology efficiently is another important aspect of teaching virtually. As the old saying goes, "have technology work for you, not you for it." There is a possibility that is not an old saying and I made it up recently. Nonetheless, make sure you are aware of all of the online websites, browser extensions, and programs that your school district pays for. Typically, your administrator or school librarian will have a list of all the online resources your district has access to. It is worth exploring and playing around with the available educational websites and programs so that you are able to lesson plan to the best extent possible. Many times, these online programs, websites, and browser extensions enhance our teaching and objectives. For example, there is currently a program that is considered a browser extension that allows for teachers to make their online class more interactive. Students can type their answers to questions that teachers develop, and teachers then have the choice to show student answers as well. This allows teachers to use a mix of verbal and nonverbal participation online. In theory, teachers can continually unmute students each time they ask a question. However, this is a huge waste of time and not every student will want to participate online. Having an interactive program to add to lessons allows all students to participate in some way. When a teacher has this mindset, they are allowing technology to "work for them," and not the other way around.

Start Small

The market for educational programs can be somewhat saturated and overwhelming. Choose two or three that you can incorporate into your online classroom and stick with those for a bit. Once you master those three programs, consider branching out and trying to learn something else. I always recommend using search engines to find premade tutorials on how to use educational programs. There are a lot of teacher-made tutorials that are very useful. If you are trying to master too many online tools at once and do not become proficient at any of them, you are then working for the technology!

Create Clear Directions and Structures

Virtual learning requires teachers to communicate even more frequently and clearly. Not teaching a class in person makes giving directions and academic feedback much more difficult. Establish structures so that your students and parents know what to expect. Set one day a week where you send an email to all parent/guardians: for example, every Friday morning you will send a recap of the week. (Figure 12.1) provides an example of what can be sent out the first Friday of a school year. After sending a recap message, you can include reminders of upcoming assignments and important dates. Parents, guardians, and students will all know to expect to hear from you each Friday morning, which opens up the communication channels.

When teaching online, state the directions out loud and type them on the document as well. Some students may have poor Wi-Fi and need to see the information in writing too.

Example Email

Dear Parent(s)/Guardian(s),

As your child's history teacher this year, I would like to introduce myself. My name is Mr. Katzel and I have taught at XXXXX School for the past four years. In addition to teaching, I serve as one of the 6th Grade Team Leaders. I am looking forward to a productive partnership with you to ensure each student will achieve their highest potential. I have the belief that by working together we will make this a very successful school year.

I invite you to email me anytime that you have a question regarding your child's progress in school. I will do my part by keeping you informed by sending a weekly message out through the XXXXX Classroom Portal. I will be assigning assignments through the "XXXX Classroom Portal". When I assign work, I will use the acronyms of "DD" and "DL". The "DD" stands for the assignment's due date. While the "DL" stands for the deadline for the assignment to be turned in. The deadline is the last day that an assignment can be completed for credit. This information can also be accessed in the modules tab in XXXX Classroom Portal when work is assigned.

Please let me know if you have any questions. I am looking forward to a great year!

Thank You,

Mr. Katzel

Figure 12.1 A example email that can be sent during online school. (An example email that a teacher can send out to parents if instruction is moved from in person to virtual. The email contains information on the structure of the class, class subject, and teacher email.)

Final Thoughts

Teaching, whether in person or virtually, is no easy task for anyone. If your instruction is currently online, or is moved online in the future, be confident that you have the tools to make your classroom successful. The world is ever changing, and so is the profession of teaching, which requires us to adapt more quickly than almost any other industry. Do not be afraid to try different types of online resources to further enhance your instruction. Remember to start small! Developing a winning system for online schooling can be done by developing consistent procedures that are comparable to ones you would use for in-person schooling. This can be done by establishing clear structures for your virtual classroom. Regardless of whether your classroom is run virtually or in person, do not forget your winning system. The winning system you develop through-out the year will allow you to teach effectively both online and in person.

Conclusion

Make it a Great Year!

I hope that this book has given you the tools to succeed in your first year of teaching middle school. You now have resources you need for the first week of school, Back to School Night, parent–teacher conferences, short-term lesson planning, long-term lesson planning, organization, and much more. Use this book as a resource throughout the year to help you. Stay consistent, stay focused on the task at hand, and focus on the goals that you have for yourself and your students. With a winning system in place, you will have the tools to fix problems that arise in the classroom in person or online. Do not be afraid to take risks and always try to remember the foundations of the winning system you build. Students may not remember a specific lesson or fact, but they do remember how teachers made them feel. You are going to have an amazing first year of teaching. The first year of teaching always goes by the quickest; enjoy being in the moment and continue building on the winning system as you grow throughout your career.

The average time a person spends as a teacher is five years! It is hard to find any other profession that has a burn out rate of five years. The reason that teaching is so difficult is because of the daily trials and tribulations that too many educators have to go through. Many people refer to your first year of teaching as the "worst," but this does not need to be the case. Using this book as a toolkit will allow you to set yourself up for success in all aspects of your classroom. Not every lesson will go according to plan, but use this as a learning experience. Do not get too down on yourself, and always remember why you got into this profession. Keep your head up and try your best. Each year that you teach is easier than the last. Never give up on your students – and, most importantly, never give up on yourself!

Appendices

Appendix A: Mentor Teacher Checklist

Mentor Teacher Checklist (Example)

Question	Evidence (Lessons, Management Strategies, etc.)
What did my mentor teacher do well?	1. Many lessons were content- and teacher-based 2. Had routine for start, middle, and end of class 3. Classroom management was consistent and clear
What could my mentor teacher improve in their classroom?	1. Create more lessons that are student-centered and promote student discourse 2. Have a clear "I do," "we do," "you do" when going over assignments 3. Make directions clearer when going over class assignments
What strategies and parts of the teachers' system could improve?	1. Have clearer expectations on what to do when a student is absent 2. Post whether or not there is homework on the board
Does my mentor teacher even have a system in place? If the teacher has a system in place, is it a winning system?	1. My mentor teacher did have a system in place. It was a winning system due to the procedures, expectations, routines, and rules that were clearly established well before my time in their classroom. It was easy for me to jump in as a guest teacher and teach the students.

Appendix B: Sample One-Pager

Date: Tuesday, September 9, 2020

Do Now: Write down your homework and then start the warm up

Homework: Ancient Civilization Reading and Questions: DD - 9/11, DL: 9/18

Objective: SWBAT: describe the 8 themes of geography

Agenda: Warm Up -> Close Read -> 8 Themes of Geography Reading/Questions -> Interactive Exit Ticket

Appendix C: Example Syllabus

Contact Information

Mr. Stephen Katzel:

6th Grade Social Studies & Team Leader

Email: Stephen.x.katzel@XXXX@XXXX.org

School Phone: 301-XXX-XXXX

Course Overview

The Goal of Sixth Grade Social Studies is to enhance student's understanding of the ancient and modern worlds. The course is designed to develop academic skills through the lens of social studies education. Critical thinking skills will be taught through throughout the school year. Students will have many chances to collaborate and interact with their peers when analyzing content.

Unit 1–Ancient History through modern analysis: (6,000 BCE –650 CE)
- Review & Overview–Themes of Geography
- The Beginnings of Civilizations
- Rise of Cities

Unit 2–Classical History (500 CE –1500 CE)
- Analysis of Citizenship
- Structures of governments
- Development of Advanced Technologies

Unit 3–Modern History (1501 CE –Present)
- Globalization
- Impact of advanced technology

Unit 4–Economics in the Modern World
- Macroeconomics
- Microeconomics

Classroom Norms

1. Put forth your best effort each class
2. Arrive to class before the bell rings
3. Arrive to class ready to learn
4. Follow beginning of class procedures
5. No bathroom passes first/last 10 minutes of class
6. Take responsibility for the quality of your work

Suggested Materials

- Sharpened pencils
- Pens
- Wireless Mouse
- Paper
- Water Bottle

Grading Policy
A - 100%-89.5%
B - 89.4%-79.5%
C - 79.4% -69.5%
D - 69.4%-59.5%
E - 59.4% & Below

GRADE CATEGORIES
60% - Formative Assessments
20% - Summative Assessments
10% - Homework
10% - 5 Paragraph Essay
        (Quarter 1 & 3 Only)
10% - Content Project
        (Quarter 2 & 4 Only)

LATE WORK
DUE DATE – day the assignment is due.
DEADLINE – last day to turn in work for credit.

Work turned in after the due date will **lose 5%.**
No work will be accepted after deadlineunless a student has **excused absences.**

Absences and Make-up work
- All necessary work must be completed while a student is absent or immediately upon return to school. Any assignments previously announced will be due on the day the student returns to school.
- All work missed because of an absence will be due **no later** than three school days after a student returns to school.
- Students are responsible to meet with the teacher to learn about missed work and missed instruction during study hall.
- Students are expected to know and make up work from any absences over the year, both excused and unexcused.
- Students can access their missing work through the "Make-Up Binder " or by emailing the teacher for a digital copy.
- Students will be allowed one day for each day of an **excused** absence to make-up work.
- If an assignment is announced in class for a future date before a student is absent, the assignment will be given during study hall once the student returns to school.
- Work missed while a student is absent from class for reasons which are **unexcused** must be discussed with the teacher at study hall.

Appendix D: Example Long-Term Planning Calendar

	Sunday	Monday	Tuesday	Wednesday	Thursday	Friday	Saturday
Unit 2- Week #1	11/8	11/9 1 Citizenship in Ancient Times!	11/10 2 Citizenship in Ancient Times!	11/11 3 (Half Day) Purpose of Ancient Governments	11/12 4 Secondary Source Analysis	11/13 5 Purpose of Government (Secondary Source Analysis) HW #1	11/14
Unit 2- Week #2	11/15	11/16 6 Traits of Citizenship	11/17 7 Mapping Ancient Middle East	11/18 8 Ancient Civilizations	11/19 9 Map Quiz	11/20 10 (Half Day) Picture Analysis	11/21
Unit 2- Week #3	11/22	11/23 11 Warring City States	11/24 12 Primary Source Analysis HW #2	11/25 No School (Thanksgiving Break)	11/26 No School (Thanksgiving Break)	11/27 No School (Thanksgiving Break)	11/28
Unit 2- Week #4	11/29	11/30 13 Class Discussion: Choose a side in Ancient Times!	12/1 14 Class Discussion: Choose a side in Ancient Times!	12/2 15 Claim and Evidence Practice	12/3 16 Claim and Evidence Practice HW #3	12/4 17 Historical Essay Prep	12/5
Unit 2- Week #5	12/6	12/7 Science Education Field Trip (Entire 6th Grade)	12/8 Science Education Field Trip (Entire 6th Grade)	12/9 Science Education Field Trip (Entire 6th Grade)	12/10 Science Education Field Trip (Entire 6th Grade)	12/11 Science Education Field Trip (Entire 6th Grade)	12/12
Unit 2- Week #6	12/13	12/14 18 Historical Essay	12/15 19 Historical Essay	12/16 20 Historical Essay	12/17 21 Historical Essay	12/18 22 Historical Essay	12/19

Winter Break	12/20	12/21	12/22	12/23	12/24	12/25	12/26
	Winter Break (No School)	Winter Break (No School)	Winter Break (No School)	Winter Break (No School)	Winter Break (No School)	Winter Break (No School)	
Winter Break	12/27	12/28	12/29	12/30	12/31	1/1	1/2
	Winter Break (No School)	Winter Break (No School)	Winter Break (No School)	Winter Break (No School)	Winter Break (No School)	Winter Break (No School)	
Unit 2- Week #7	1/3	1/4 23 Inventions of the Ancient World	1/5 24 Impact of Technology HW #4	1/6 25 Social Class Analysis	1/7 26 Social Class Analysis	1/8 27 Impact of War	1/9
Unit 2- Week #8	1/10	1/11 28 Class Discussion: Art Analysis	1/12 29 Class Discussion: Art Analysis	1/13 30 Thesis Statement	1/14 31 Paragraph Activity- Thesis Statement Practice	1/15 32 Start of Rebellions	1/16
Unit 2- Week #9	1/17	1/18 No School (MLK Day)	1/19 33 Impact of Rebellions	1/20 34 Review Day	1/21 35 Test	1/22 36 Review Common Errors on Test	1/23
Unit 2- Week #10	1/24	1/25 37 Webquest	1/26 38 Webquest	1/27 39 Article Analysis	1/28 40 Article Analysis	1/29 41 (Half Day) Newspaper Article	1/30

Appendix E: Example Folder Organization for Lesson Plans

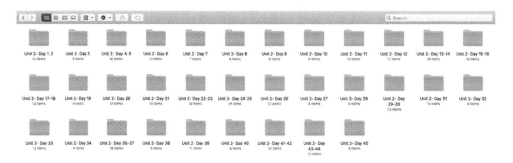

Appendix F: Sample Lesson Plan

Sample Lesson Plan: 6th Grade Social Studies

Teacher: Mr. Katzel	Grade/Subject: 6th Grade Social Studies	Unit/Day of Unit: Unit 1, Day 2
Periods: 1, 2, 6, 7	Previous Learning: 1. Analyzed maps of Europe 2. Geography of the Middle East	State Standards: GEO159- Describe human and physical characteristics by analyzing maps and other secondary sources
Academic Vocabulary: Human Geography, Physical Geography, human characteristics, physical characteristics	Daily Objective (In student Friendly Language): SWBAT (Students will be able to): Identify human and physical characteristics by analyzing maps and other secondary sources	Essential Question: Why do maps change?
Warm Up/Introduction: "Analyze a Map" Worksheet	Exit Ticket/Summarization: On the classroom portal, there will be questions on geography that are multiple choice.	Lesson Timing (Estimation in Minutes) 1. Warm-Up (5) 2. Geography Reading Close Read (5) 3. Map Analysis (15) 4. Secondary Source Analysis (15) 5. Review "Secondary Source Analysis" (5) 6. Exit Card on Geography (15)

Appendix G: Sample Parent/Teacher Conference Checklist

Teacher: Mr. Katzel, 6th Grade Team Leader & Social Studies	Email: step hen.X.XXX XXX@_____ ___.com	School Phone: 209-XXX-XXXX	Student Name: John Doe	Q1 Grade: 92% (A) Formative Grade Percentage- 90% Summative Grade Percentage – 95% Homework Grade Percentage- 100% Essay Grade Percentage- 90%
Strengths 1. Asks for help/clarification 2. Comes to class on time 3. Comes prepared with materials	Area(s) to Discuss 1. Turning in homework on time	Action Steps for Success 1. Weekly check in from Mr. Katzel by email 2. Check assignments on the online portal	Action Steps for Success 3. Write down the homework each day in the student planner	Notes:

Appendix H: Sample Page for "Back to School" Night

Welcome to Back to School Night!

Greetings Parents and Guardians! My name is Mr. Katzel and I will be your student's Social Studies teacher for the 20XX-20XX school year! This will be my 8th year teaching and I am looking forward to working with you!

Appendix I: Sample Salary Scale

Example of a Salary Scale

Salary Step (Years of Experience)	Bachelor's Degree	Master's Degree	Master's Degree + 30 graduate credits	Master's Degree + 60 graduate credits
1	$47,000	$51,000	$52,000	$54,500
10	$57,000	$64,980	$67,260	$68,970

Appendix J: Sample Email

Email Title: Welcome Back to XXXXXX Middle School and to Mr. Katzel's Class!

Dear Parent(s)/Guardian(s),

As your child's history teacher this year, I would like to introduce myself. My name is Mr. Katzel and I have taught at XXXX Middle School for the past four years. In addition to \teaching, I serve as one of the Team Leaders.

I have a strong belief that a partnership between teachers and parent/guardians leads to students achieving their highest potential. By working together, we are going to make this a rememberable year! I invite you to email me anytime that you have a question regarding your child's progress in school.

I will be assigning assignments through the "XXXX Classroom Portal". When I assign work, I will use the acronyms of "DD" and "DL". The "DD" stands for the assignment's due date. While the "DL" stands for the deadline for the assignment to be turned in. The deadline is the last day that an assignment can be completed for credit.

Please let me know if you have any questions. I am looking forward to a great year!

Thank You,

Mr. Katzel

Appendix K: Interview Assignment

<u>**Name**</u>   <u>**Date**</u>   <u>**Period**</u>

<u>Interview Form</u>

<u>Name of person who is being interviewed:</u>

1. What is one goal that you have for the 20XX-20XX school year?

2. What was your favorite part of summer vacation?

3. In your opinion, what is the best way to achieve a goal in school?

<u>Name of person who is being interviewed:</u>

1. What is one goal that you have for the 20XX-20XX school year?

2. What was your favorite part of summer vacation?

3. In your opinion, what is the best way to achieve a goal in school?

<u>Name of person who is being interviewed:</u>

1. What is one goal that you have for the 20XX-20XX school year?

2. What was your favorite part of summer vacation?

3. In your opinion, what is the best way to achieve a goal in school?

Appendix L: 5 Themes of Geography Assignment

<u>8.Themes of Geography Discussion</u>

Name: Group 1 or 2 (Circle)

<u>Question</u>	<u>Answer (3-4 sentences)</u>	<u>Question(s) for the Class</u>
1. How does geography impact your life?		
2. Which theme of geography is the most important? Please explain.		
3. Which theme of geography is the least important? Please explain.		

Appendix M: Observation Checklist

Socratic Seminar Observation Checklist

Your Name: Partner's Name:

Put a tally mark each time your partner..	Notes about the Discussion
Speaks in the discussion:	
Refers to the article:	
Asks a question to a classmate:	
Responds to another speaker:	

Appendix N: First Week of School –Autobiography

First Week of School-Autobiography

Name_____   Date_____

Question	How would you describe yourself using one word?	How would you describe yourself as a student in 2-3 sentences?	What is a challenge that you have overcome in your life?	What does success in seventh grade look like to you?
Answer				

Appendix O: End of Semester –Autobiography

End of First Semester-Autobiography

Name_____   Date_____

Question	How would you describe yourself using one word?	How would you describe yourself in 2-3 sentences? Is this similar or different than what you put at the start of the year?	What is a challenge that you have overcome in the first semester of school?	How have you changed as a student since the first day of seventh grade?
Answer				

Appendix P: Example Exit Ticket

Name: _____ Date: _____
Period: _____
Choice: _____

<u>Student Choice Exit Ticket</u>

Directions: You may choose ONE of the two options below to show your learning. You do NOT have to complete both assignments. Use the next page to complete one of the assignments below.

1. Social Media Page—Make a social media profile for a historical figure during the British colonization of the United States. Your profile must have at least 2 the following 5 vocabulary terms mentioned on the page: King, Monarchy, Stamp Act, Trade, Famine. You can choose the location/time of the profile.

2. Cartoon—Draw a cartoon summarizing a day in the life of an American colonist after spending their first month in one of the colonies.

Appendix Q: Collapse of Soviet Union Assignment

Collapse of the Soviet Union

Name: **Date:**   **Period:**

The year is 1991 and the Soviet Union just fell apart. 14 new countries just broke apart from the Soviet Union and you have to think fast. As the leader of the new <u>democratic</u> Russia you have a lot of decisions to make. The United States has reached out to you and offered their help. Now the question is do you trust them?

The first step you have is to figure out things about your own country before deciding what you are going to do.

1. What is your countries name?
   Russia or come up with a new name

2. 14 new countries broke apart from the Soviet Union. Should Russia try to get them to become part of the new Russia? Explain your reasoning.

3. What is the capital of non-communist Russia? (Come up with the name)

4. Now that communism is gone how soon will you decide to start elections to elect leaders? Should elections be right away? Should they be in a year so that the country has time to organize?

5. Should you accept help from communist China even though you are the leader of the new non-communist Russia?

6. What should the new democratic government do with the ole communist leaders? Should they be jailed or allowed to live freely? Explain your reasoning.

7. The United States has reached out and offered to help your country since you are no longer communist. Should the United States be an ally now that Russia is democratic and not communist? Explain your reasoning by citing reasons from what you have learned in class. (Answer in a paragraph of at least 7 sentences)

Appendix R: Budget Activity

Name_____

Budget Activity- Economic Depression

The month is February (a non-leap year) and there are 28 days you need to make a budget for! You have a tight budget for the month! You have $19.87 in your bank account and just got paid from work. Your paycheck just gave you $8.49 after taxes. This is where is gets tricky! This means that you have $28.36 to spend in the next month. You have to provide shelter, food, and water for your family. Your family consists of you, your brother, and two parents. Rent is due at the end of the month, and it costs $7 and must be paid on time. If you do not fill your car up with gas, you will have to walk 4 miles to work. Please items choose wisely!

1. Rent- $7
2. Milk- $2
3. Eggs (Enough for 1 week)- $.91
4. .5 Pound of Chicken Tenders- $.54
5. .5 Pound of Ground Beef- $.71
6. Electric Bill- $3.45
7. Cost of gas to fill up your car for a week- $1.24
8. Flour (For 2 pounds)- $2.34
9. Bag of Rice (10 Pounds)- $3.19
10. One Pound of Coffee (Enough for a month)- $3.42
11. Potatoes (2 Pounds)- $2.41
12. Bicycle- $5.68

***Please show all of your "math" work on the back of the paper.**

Made in the USA
Columbia, SC
14 July 2022

63451234R00054